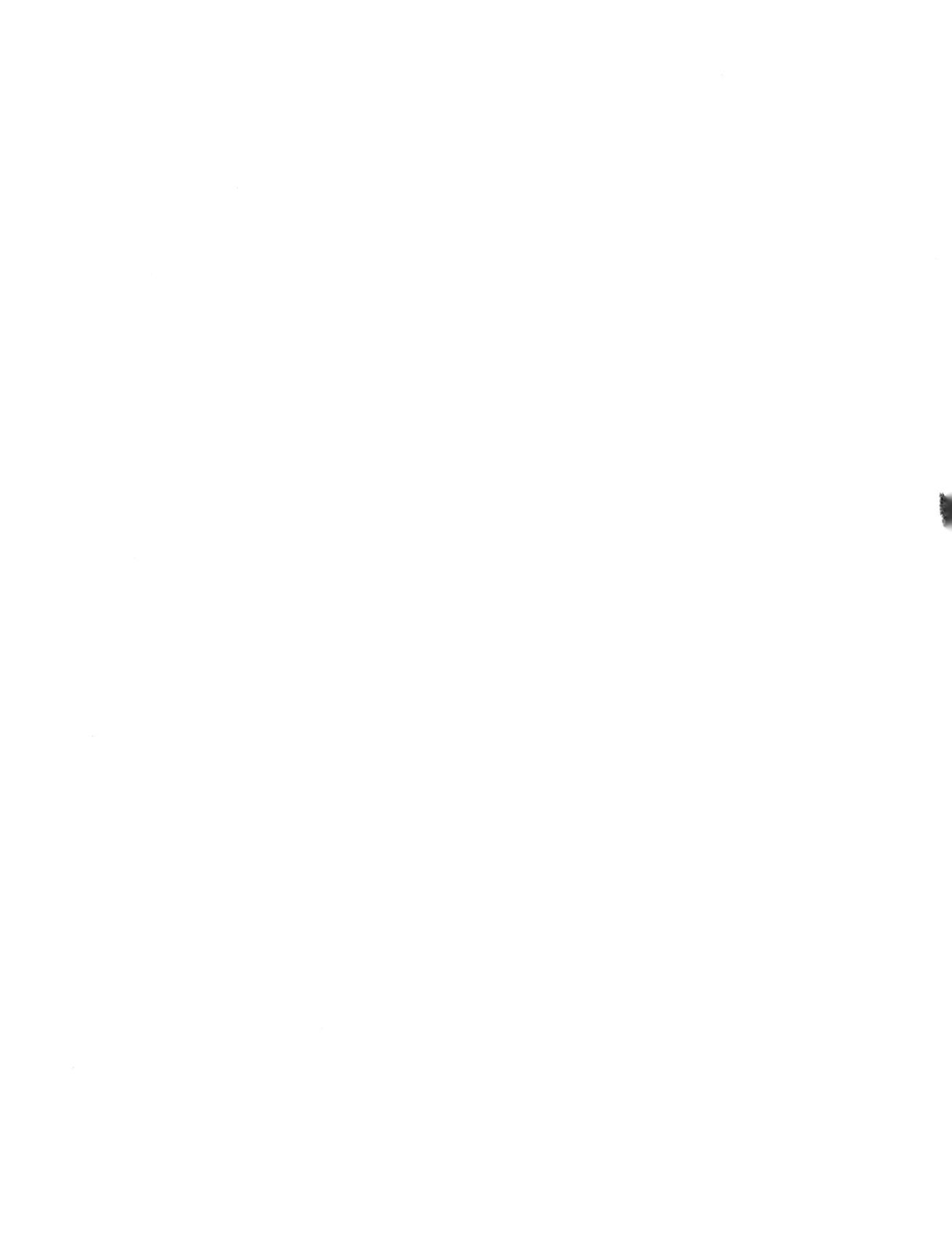

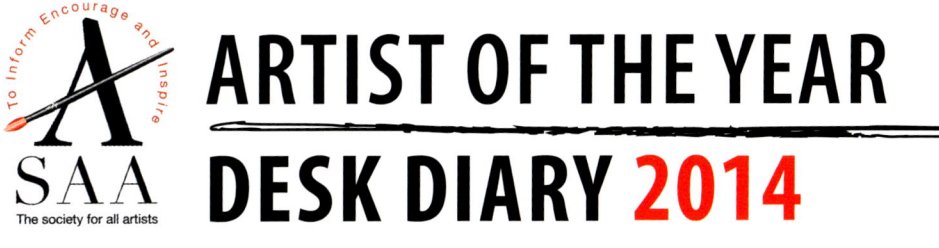

# ARTIST OF THE YEAR
## DESK DIARY 2014

 *Welcome to the 'Artist of the Year' Desk Diary – brought to you in association with the SAA, society for all artists.*

Featuring over 50 stunning, award winning entries from the SAA 2013 'Artist of the Year' Competition – this beautiful week-to-view desk diary is packed with some of the most popular styles, subjects and mediums that combine to celebrate the very best of artistic abilities.

### Unlock your creativity with the SAA…

Whether you're a beginner, improver or professional – discover how we can encourage and inspire you to try something new.

Visit us at **www.saa.co.uk** or call **0800 980 1123** and discover how we can help you network with thousands of other like-minded artists and help unlock your creative passion.

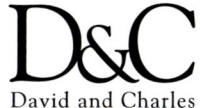

www.stitchcraftcreate.co.uk

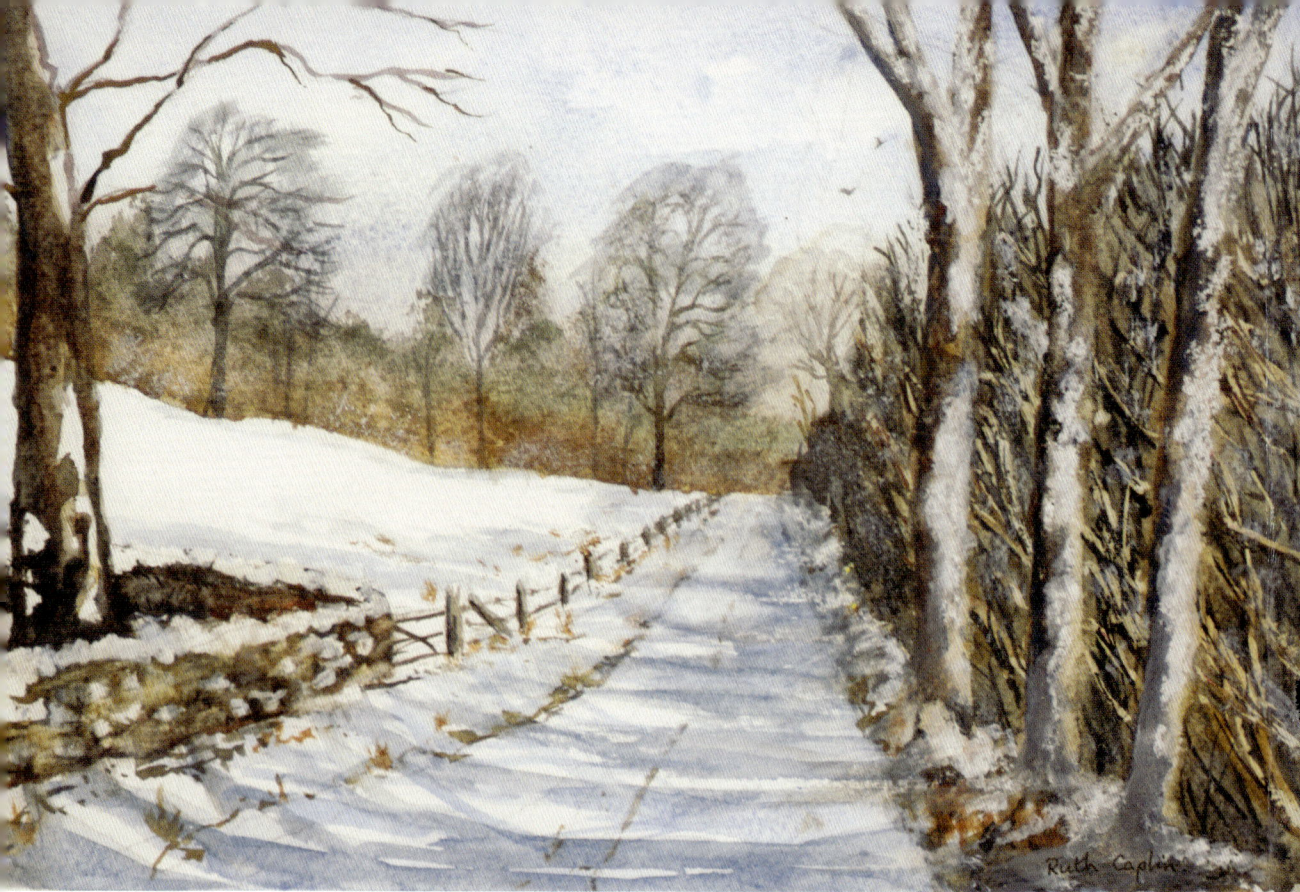

Best Beginner in the Landscape or Woodland Scene Category

## The Road Home
### Ruth Caplin
Mixed Media

" On the Yorkshire Moors we had heavy snowfall this winter. I find snow inspiring in the way it transforms the landscape and coats the trees and stone walls around here. I have a particular fondness for the field on the left of the picture; it is where crowds of us roll our hard-boiled eggs down its slopes at Easter. I enjoyed painting this and was particularly pleased with the sunlight on the thicket at the right. "

# December /January

30
Monday

31
Tuesday

*New Year's Day*

1
Wednesday

2
Thursday

3
Friday

4
Saturday

5
Sunday

| JANUARY | | | | | | |
|---|---|---|---|---|---|---|
| M | T | W | T | F | S | S |
|  |  | 1 | 2 | 3 | 4 | 5 |
| 6 | 7 | 8 | 9 | 10 | 11 | 12 |
| 13 | 14 | 15 | 16 | 17 | 18 | 19 |
| 20 | 21 | 22 | 23 | 24 | 25 | 26 |
| 27 | 28 | 29 | 30 | 31 |  |  |

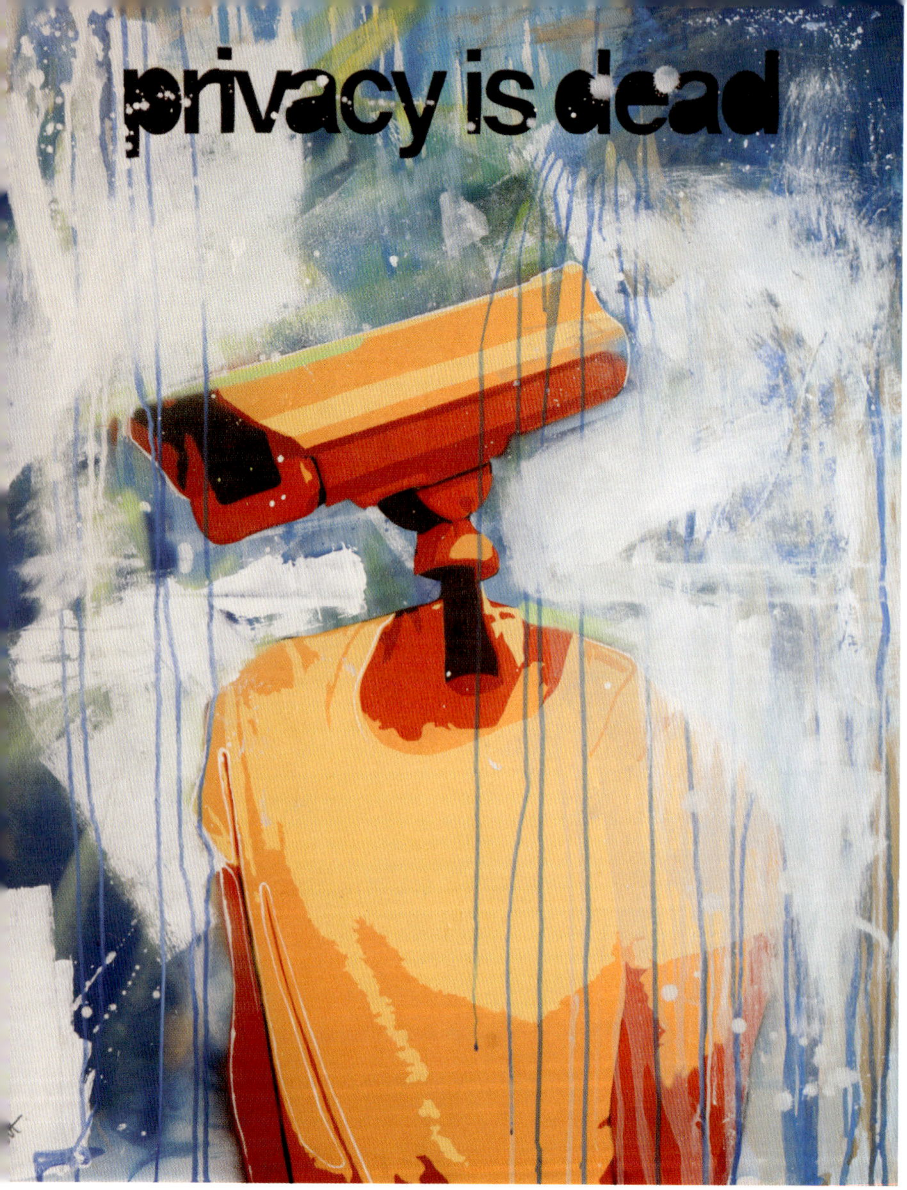

# privacy is dead

Best Young in the Abstract or Experimental Category

## Privacy Is Dead
**William Alexander**

*Mixed Media*

> This painting represents the concept of the Big Brother Nation, loss of privacy, and the CCTV cameras that watch us. Influenced by artists including Banksy and Dolk, I combined then edited images prior to stencilling. The background was created by freehand spray painting, rolling and flicking acrylic paint, then the image was integrated with more loose work on top. By utilising scale, contrasting colours and a strong graphic image, I hope to grab viewers' attention.

www.fortelondon.co.uk

# January

## 6
Monday

## 7
Tuesday

## 8
Wednesday

## 9
Thursday

## 10
Friday

## 11
Saturday

## 12
Sunday

| **JANUARY** | | | | | | |
|---|---|---|---|---|---|---|
| M | T | W | T | F | S | S |
| | | 1 | 2 | 3 | 4 | 5 |
| 6 | 7 | 8 | 9 | 10 | 11 | 12 |
| 13 | 14 | 15 | 16 | 17 | 18 | 19 |
| 20 | 21 | 22 | 23 | 24 | 25 | 26 |
| 27 | 28 | 29 | 30 | 31 | | |

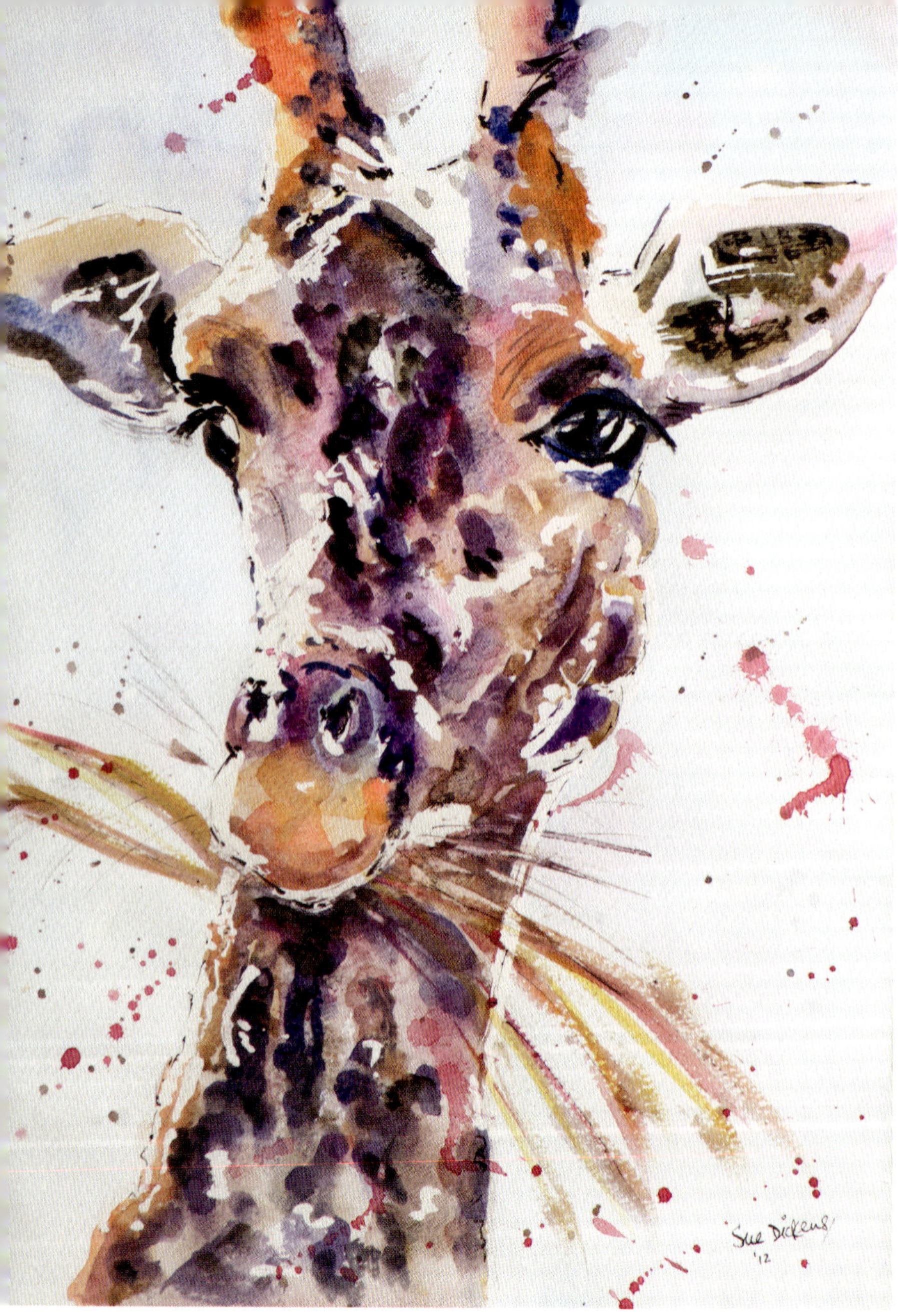

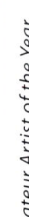

*Amateur Artist of the Year*

# Giraffe

*Sue Dickens*

Watercolour

Entering was a spur of the moment thing at the very last minute. The most difficult aspect of the painting was emulating the soft texture of the giraffe's fur, and of course the eyes. I love the informal aspect of this painting style and my work seems to be moving in this direction. As an amateur I have a long way to go and am learning something new every day.

www.suedickens.com

# January

**13**
Monday

**14**
Tuesday

**15**
Wednesday

**16**
Thursday

**17**
Friday

**18**
Saturday

**19**
Sunday

| JANUARY | | | | | | |
|---|---|---|---|---|---|---|
| M | T | W | T | F | S | S |
|  |  | 1 | 2 | 3 | 4 | 5 |
| 6 | 7 | 8 | 9 | 10 | 11 | 12 |
| 13 | 14 | 15 | 16 | 17 | 18 | 19 |
| 20 | 21 | 22 | 23 | 24 | 25 | 26 |
| 27 | 28 | 29 | 30 | 31 |  |  |

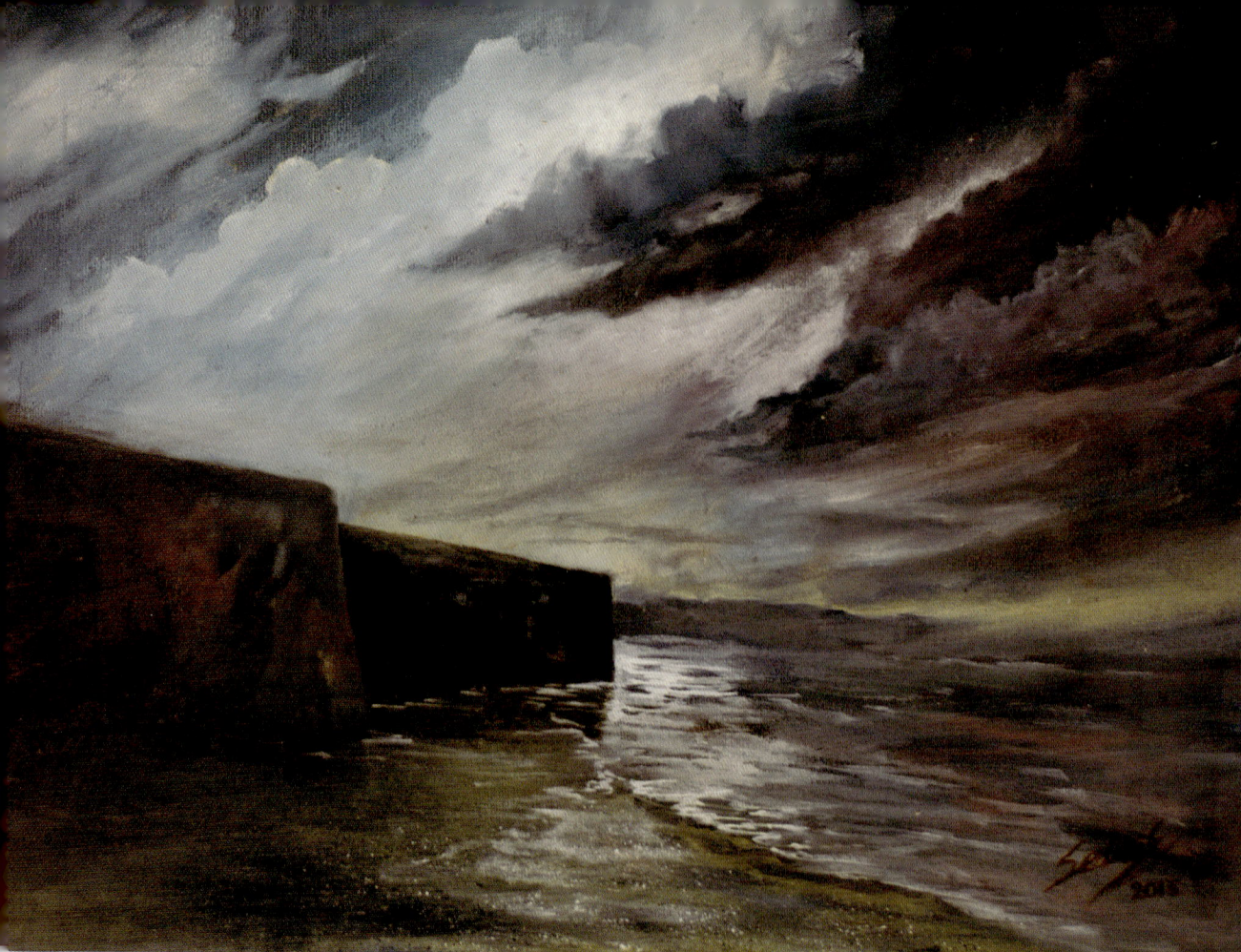

## Manningtree Beach

*Best Young in the Waterscape, Boats or Seascape Category*

### Sam Lucas

Oils

> Watching the local annual regatta on the shore of the River Stour, I was struck by the amazing, powerful cloud formations above us. I committed these to memory and did a quick sketch as soon as I got home. I like to try and encompass power and emotion into my work where possible, and feel this is one of the best examples.

# January

*Martin Luther King Day (US)*

**20**
Monday

**21**
Tuesday

**22**
Wednesday

**23**
Thursday

**24**
Friday

**25**
Saturday

*Australia Day (Aus)*

**26**
Sunday

| **JANUARY** | | | | | | |
|---|---|---|---|---|---|---|
| M | T | W | T | F | S | S |
|  |  | 1 | 2 | 3 | 4 | 5 |
| 6 | 7 | 8 | 9 | 10 | 11 | 12 |
| 13 | 14 | 15 | 16 | 17 | 18 | 19 |
| 20 | 21 | 22 | 23 | 24 | 25 | 26 |
| 27 | 28 | 29 | 30 | 31 |  |  |

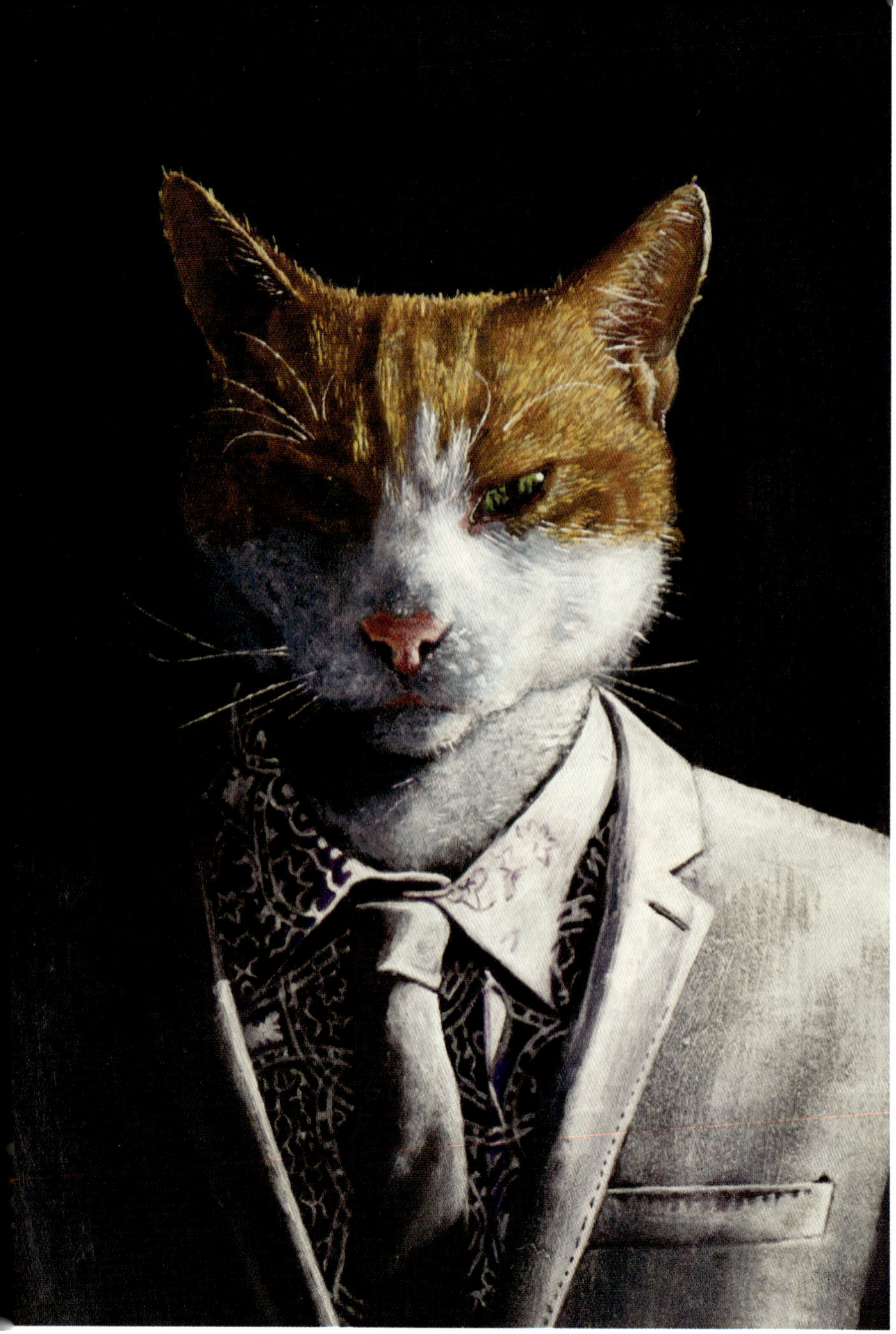

*Young Artist of the Year*

## Basil

### Daniel Connolly

*Acrylics*

This unusual pet portrait is of one of my three cats, Basil. I wanted to translate my cat's personality and character into a piece, with his sly expression, his piercing eyes and his ginger fur against the purple shirt. The smart suit represents the many hours he spends every day grooming himself.

# January/February

**27** Monday

**28** Tuesday

**29** Wednesday

**30** Thursday

*Chinese New Year*

**31** Friday

**1** Saturday

**2** Sunday

| | | | JANUARY | | | |
|---|---|---|---|---|---|---|
| M | T | W | T | F | S | S |
| | | | | 1 | 2 | 3 |
| 4 | 5 | | | | | |
| 6 | 7 | 8 | 9 | 10 | 11 | 12 |
| 13 | 14 | 15 | 16 | 17 | 18 | 19 |
| 20 | 21 | 22 | 23 | 24 | 25 | 26 |
| 27 | 28 | 29 | 30 | 31 | | |

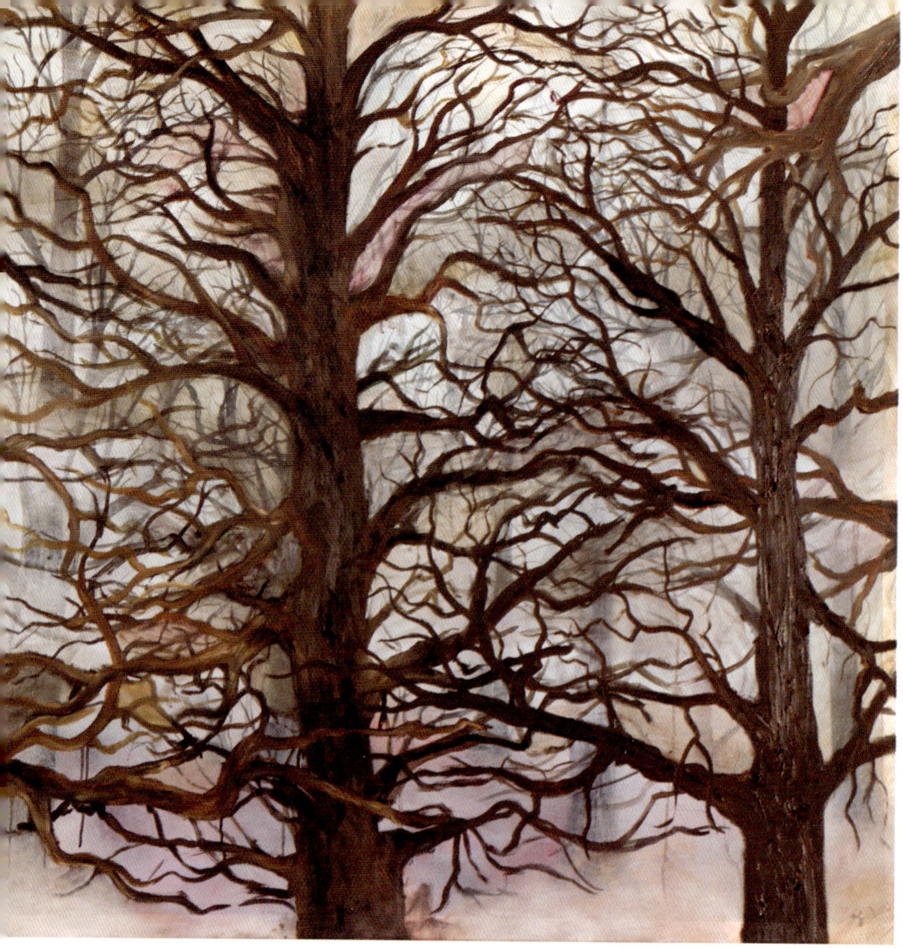

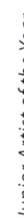

*Junior Artist of the Year*

# Woodland Study I
*Jordan Verdes*

Oils

" This painting was inspired by an image I found whilst looking for a screensaver. When I started the painting I was using techniques learnt from an artist called Wilson Bickford. Working in layers I slowly built up the image, and was inspired in the last week of the painting's completion by the works of Piet Mondrian. The most difficult thing was knowing when to stop. It was my first large scale painting and my first adventure with oil colour. "

# February

### 3
Monday

### 4
Tuesday

### 5
Wednesday

### 6
Thursday

### 7
Friday

### 8
Saturday

### 9
Sunday

**FEBRUARY**

| M | T | W | T | F | S | S |
|---|---|---|---|---|---|---|
|   |   |   |   |   | 1 | 2 |
| 3 | 4 | 5 | 6 | 7 | 8 | 9 |
| 10 | 11 | 12 | 13 | 14 | 15 | 16 |
| 17 | 18 | 19 | 20 | 21 | 22 | 23 |
| 24 | 25 | 26 | 27 | 28 |   |   |

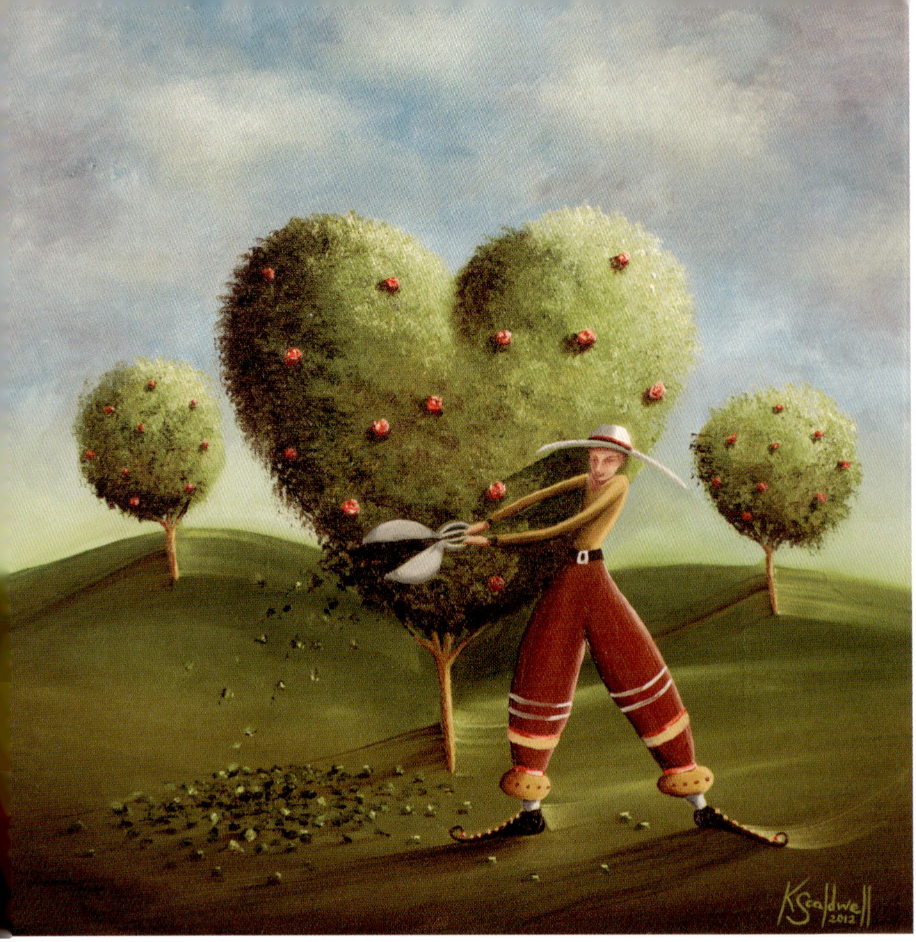

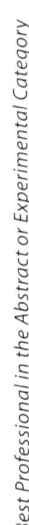

*Best Professional in the Abstract or Experimental Category*

## Tree Of Life

*Kathryn Scaldwell Culf*

Oils

> The *Tree Of Life* shows a gardener trimming a simple tree into a beautiful heart shape, making it stand out from the other trees, and revealing its true beauty. The message in this painting is one of love and identity. People believe they are plain and nothing special, but there is a beauty within them. To show love, and to love broken hearts back to life, can be the most rewarding gift anyone can give.

www.kathrynscaldwell.com

# February

**10**
Monday

**11**
Tuesday

**12**
Wednesday

**13**
Thursday

*Valentine's Day*

**14**
Friday

**15**
Saturday

**16**
Sunday

**FEBRUARY**

| M | T | W | T | F | S | S |
|---|---|---|---|---|---|---|
|   |   |   |   |   | 1 | 2 |
| 3 | 4 | 5 | 6 | 7 | 8 | 9 |
| 10 | 11 | 12 | 13 | 14 | 15 | 16 |
| 17 | 18 | 19 | 20 | 21 | 22 | 23 |
| 24 | 25 | 26 | 27 | 28 |   |   |

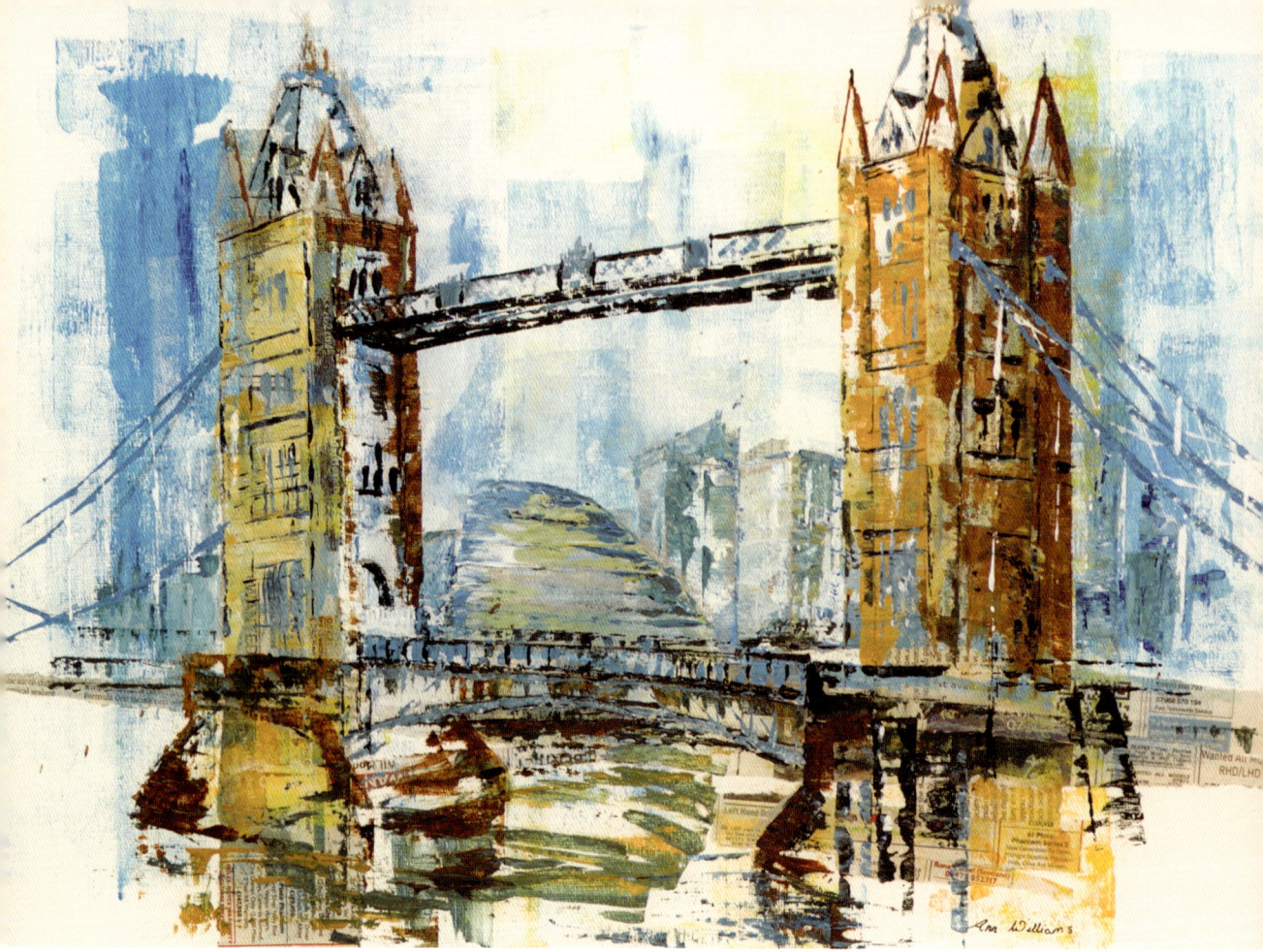

*Best Amateur in the Landscape or Woodland Scene*

## City Landmarks, Old And New
### Ann Williams
*Acrylics and Mixed Media*

> *City Landmarks, Old and New* was inspired by a personal photograph taken along the Thames Pathway. I was intrigued by the smooth curves of City Hall visible through the strong uprights and lines of Tower Bridge. I enjoy the freedom and uncertainty of working with acrylics using rollers, old credit cards and finally a palette knife for details and structure. The photograph is used as a starting point, then I follow my instincts.

www.annwilliams.co.uk

# February

*Presidents' Day (US)*

**17** Monday

**18** Tuesday

**19** Wednesday

**20** Thursday

**21** Friday

**22** Saturday

**23** Sunday

| **FEBRUARY** | | | | | | |
|---|---|---|---|---|---|---|
| M | T | W | T | F | S | S |
|  |  |  |  |  | 1 | 2 |
| 3 | 4 | 5 | 6 | 7 | 8 | 9 |
| 10 | 11 | 12 | 13 | 14 | 15 | 16 |
| 17 | 18 | 19 | 20 | 21 | 22 | 23 |
| 24 | 25 | 26 | 27 | 28 |  |  |

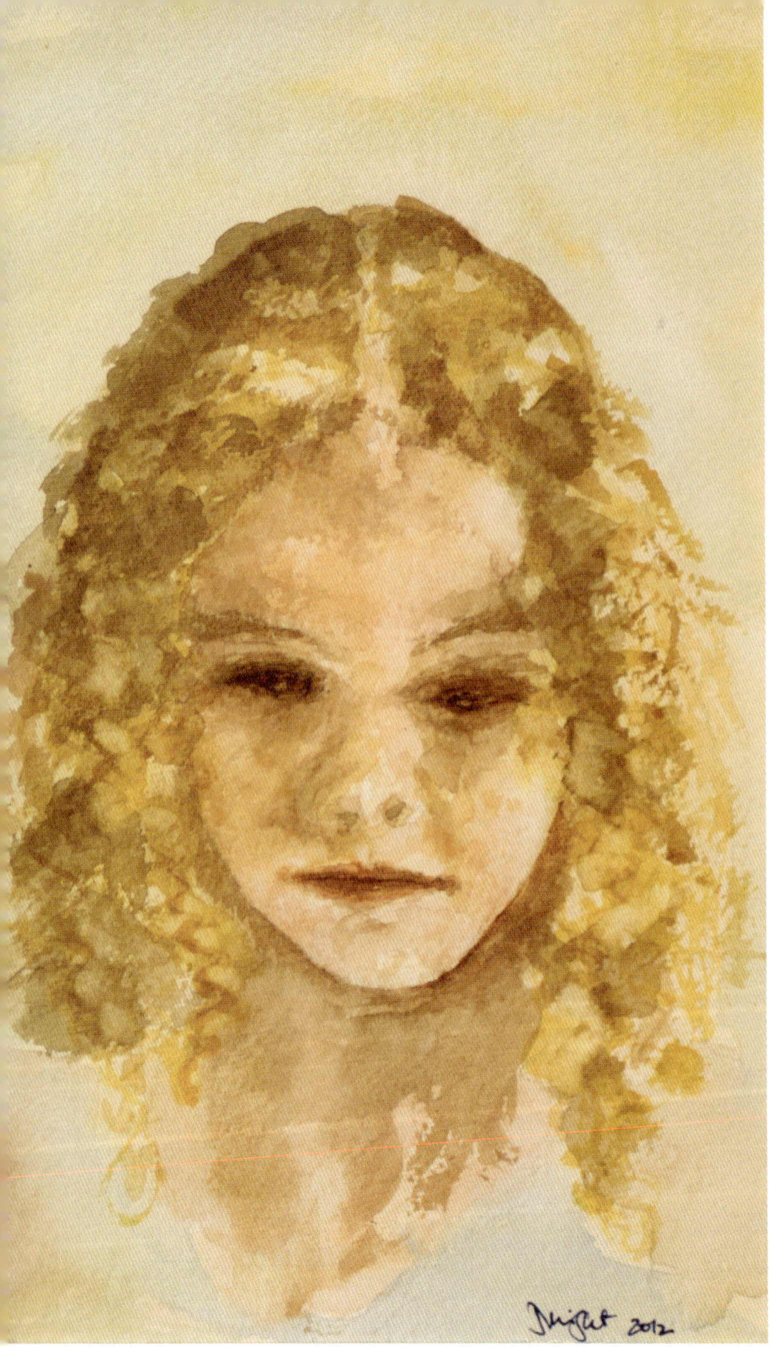

*Best Beginner in the Portrait or Figure Category*

## Nina, Aged 6
### John Wright
*Watercolour*

" I took a photograph of Nina, my 6 year old granddaughter, at my stepson's wedding last summer, and I decided to use it to paint this picture to include in her birthday card as a surprise. Fortunately she loves it and the picture now hangs in her bedroom, so I'll now have to work my way through the other grandchildren! "

www.johnwright101.tumblr.com

# February/March

**24**
Monday

**25**
Tuesday

**26**
Wednesday

**27**
Thursday

**28**
Friday

**1**
Saturday

**2**
Sunday

**FEBRUARY**

| M | T | W | T | F | S | S |
|---|---|---|---|---|---|---|
|   |   |   |   |   | 1 | 2 |
| 3 | 4 | 5 | 6 | 7 | 8 | 9 |
| 10 | 11 | 12 | 13 | 14 | 15 | 16 |
| 17 | 18 | 19 | 20 | 21 | 22 | 23 |
| 24 | 25 | 26 | 27 | 28 |   |   |

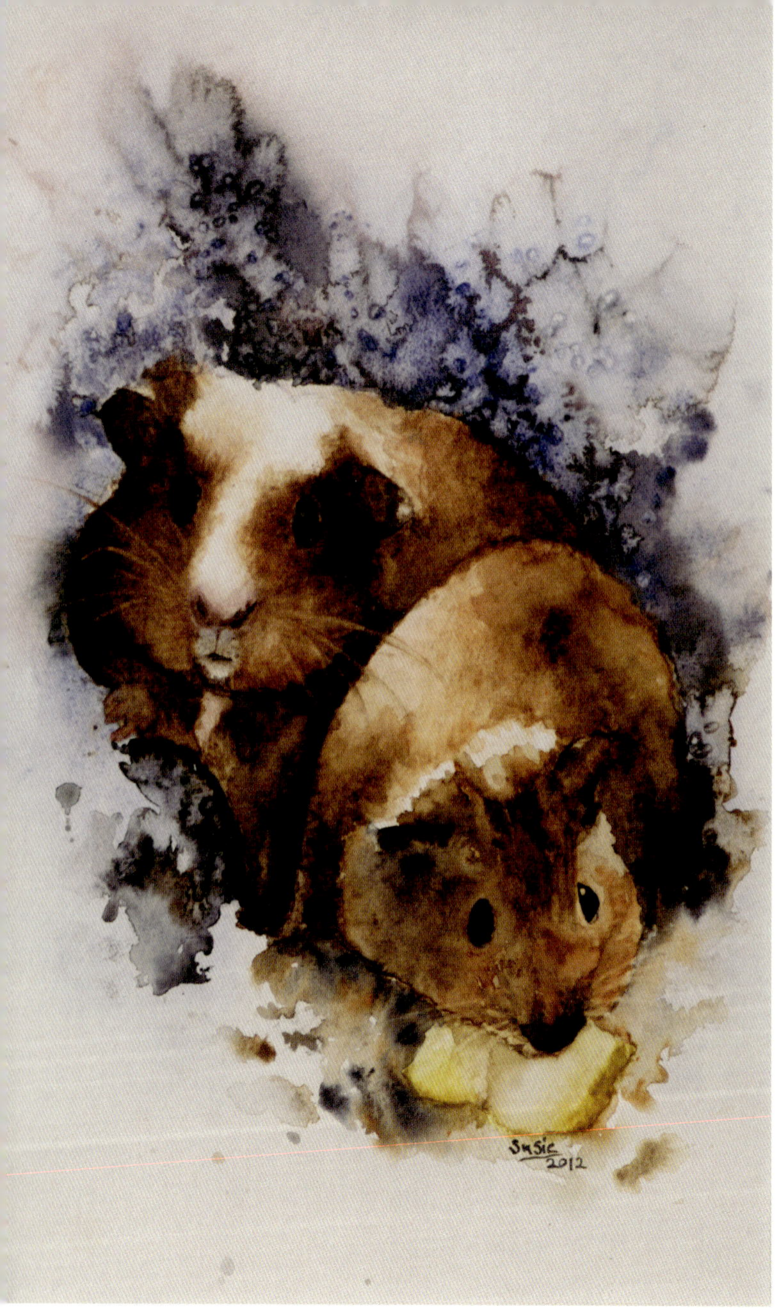

*Best Junior in the Animal or Wildlife Category*

# Guinea Pigs
## Susie Exley
*Watercolour*

"This was a commission painted for a friend's birthday. I took photos of the guinea pigs while they were eating some apple. In fact one escaped and hid for a while! I used watercolour and salt for the background, and was pleased with the colour combinations of Payne's grey and ultramarine, which contrasted with the burnt sienna and ochre of the guinea pigs. The textured effect of the salt worked well – luckily!"

# March

## 3
### Monday

*Shrove Tuesday*

## 4
### Tuesday

## 5
### Wednesday

## 6
### Thursday

## 7
### Friday

## 8
### Saturday

## 9
### Sunday

| **MARCH** | | | | | | |
|---|---|---|---|---|---|---|
| **M** | **T** | **W** | **T** | **F** | **S** | **S** |
| | | | | | 1 | 2 |
| 3 | 4 | 5 | 6 | 7 | 8 | 9 |
| 10 | 11 | 12 | 13 | 14 | 15 | 16 |
| 17 | 18 | 19 | 20 | 21 | 22 | 23 |
| 24 | 25 | 26 | 27 | 28 | 29 | 30 |
| 31 | | | | | | |

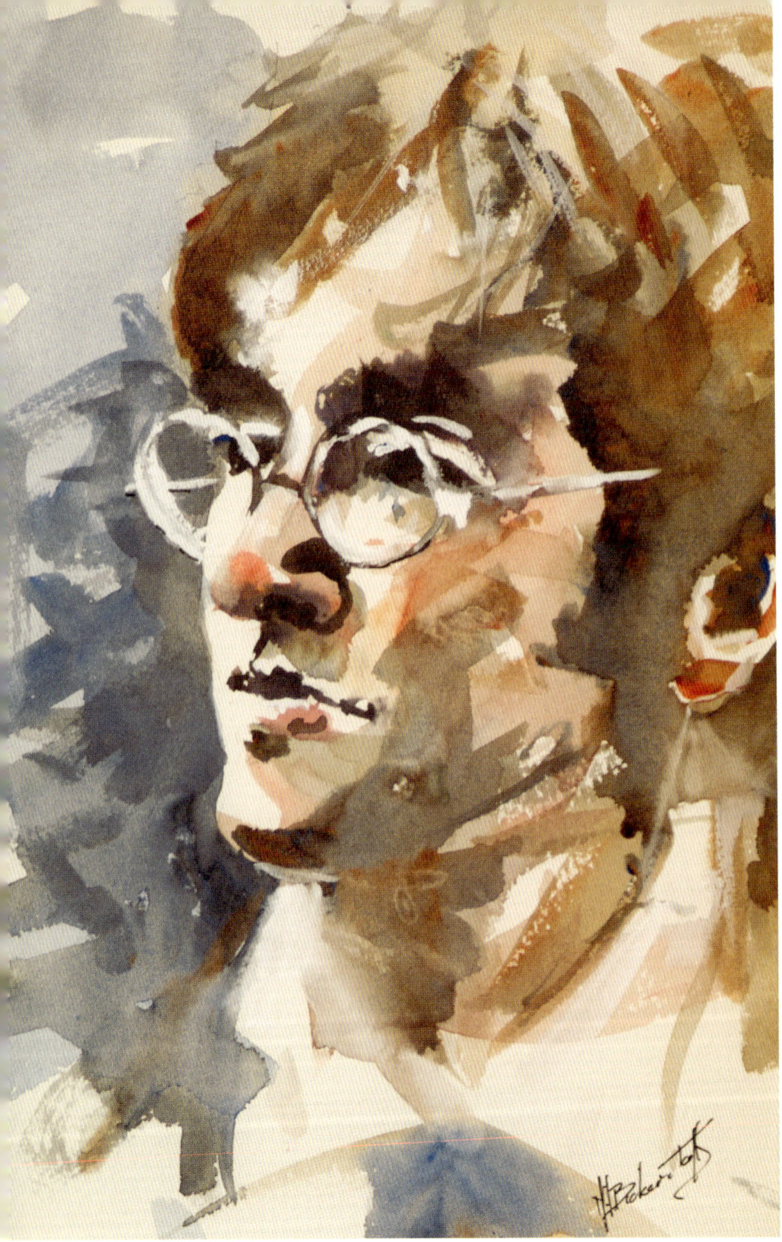

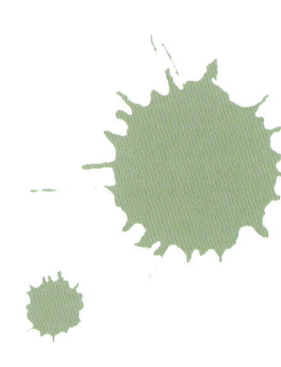

*Best Amateur in the Portrait or Figure Category*

# Legend

## *Jim Bickerstaffe*

*Watercolour*

A very quick painting done on 140lb sketchbook paper at a local art club evening meeting, not at the time intended for exhibitions or publication. I made a simple pencil sketch first, which I normal do with portraits, then I worked quickly, some wet in wet; when dry, I added a dark wash and gouache body colour to the glasses. I was pleased that it seemed to work first time. The contrast in the photo made me want to paint it.

# March

**10**
Monday

**11**
Tuesday

**12**
Wednesday

**13**
Thursday

**14**
Friday

**15**
Saturday

**16**
Sunday

| | | | MARCH | | | |
|---|---|---|---|---|---|---|
| M | T | W | T | F | S | S |
| | | | | | 1 | 2 |
| 3 | 4 | 5 | 6 | 7 | 8 | 9 |
| 10 | 11 | 12 | 13 | 14 | 15 | 16 |
| 17 | 18 | 19 | 20 | 21 | 22 | 23 |
| 24 | 25 | 26 | 27 | 28 | 29 | 30 |
| 31 | | | | | | |

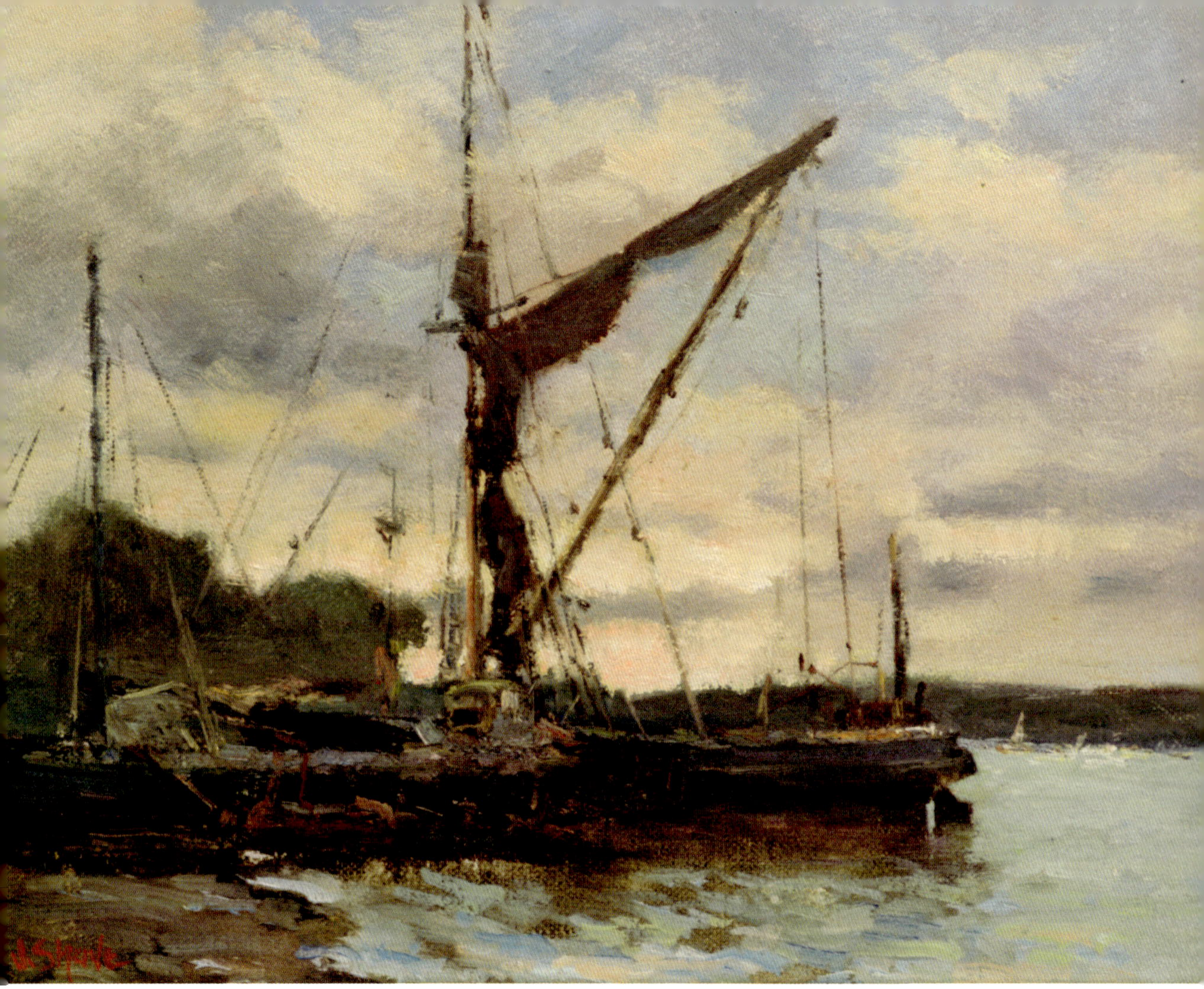

## Evening Pin Mill
### John Shave
Oils

*Best Professional in the Waterscape, Boats or Seascape Category*

> Pin Mill on the River Orwell is one of my favourite places. This painting was completed on site, late on in the afternoon. The day had been overcast but the light changed at the end of the day, as it often does, leaving the scene before me quiet and peaceful, with the light in the distance leaving the boats in silhouette. My favourite and most inspirational time of day.

www.johnshave.co.uk

# March

*St Patrick's Day*

**17**
Monday

**18**
Tuesday

**19**
Wednesday

**20**
Thursday

**21**
Friday

**22**
Saturday

**23**
Sunday

### MARCH

| M | T | W | T | F | S | S |
|---|---|---|---|---|---|---|
|   |   |   |   |   | 1 | 2 |
| 3 | 4 | 5 | 6 | 7 | 8 | 9 |
| 10 | 11 | 12 | 13 | 14 | 15 | 16 |
| 17 | 18 | 19 | 20 | 21 | 22 | 23 |
| 24 | 25 | 26 | 27 | 28 | 29 | 30 |
| 31 |   |   |   |   |   |   |

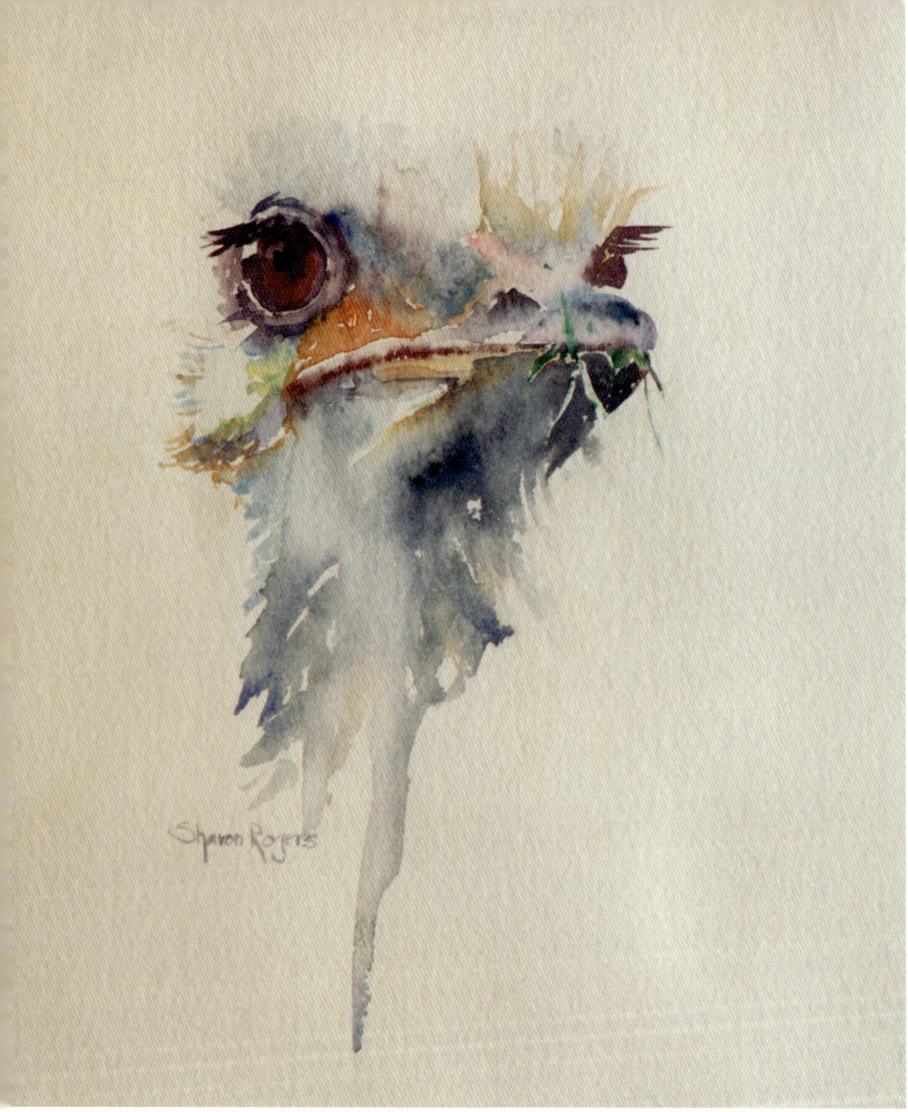

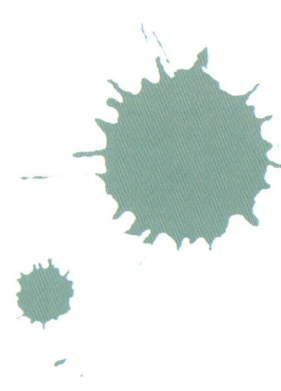

*Best Professional in the Animal or Wildlife Category*

# I Have Attitude
*Sharon Rogers*

Watercolour

 This ostrich lives at Marwell Zoo, and from the moment he glared at me from behind his fence, I knew I had to paint him. After taking several photos, the one I chose showed the most attitude. I started the painting with his eye (on the left) by adding and mixing paint on the paper, then just continued outwards until he appeared.

www.facebook.com/sharonrogersartist

# March

## 24
Monday

## 25
Tuesday

## 26
Wednesday

## 27
Thursday

## 28
Friday

## 29
Saturday

*Mother's Day (UK)*

## 30
Sunday

| **MARCH** | | | | | | |
|---|---|---|---|---|---|---|
| M | T | W | T | F | S | S |
|  |  |  |  |  | 1 | 2 |
| 3 | 4 | 5 | 6 | 7 | 8 | 9 |
| 10 | 11 | 12 | 13 | 14 | 15 | 16 |
| 17 | 18 | 19 | 20 | 21 | 22 | 23 |
| 24 | 25 | 26 | 27 | 28 | 29 | 30 |
| 31 |  |  |  |  |  |  |

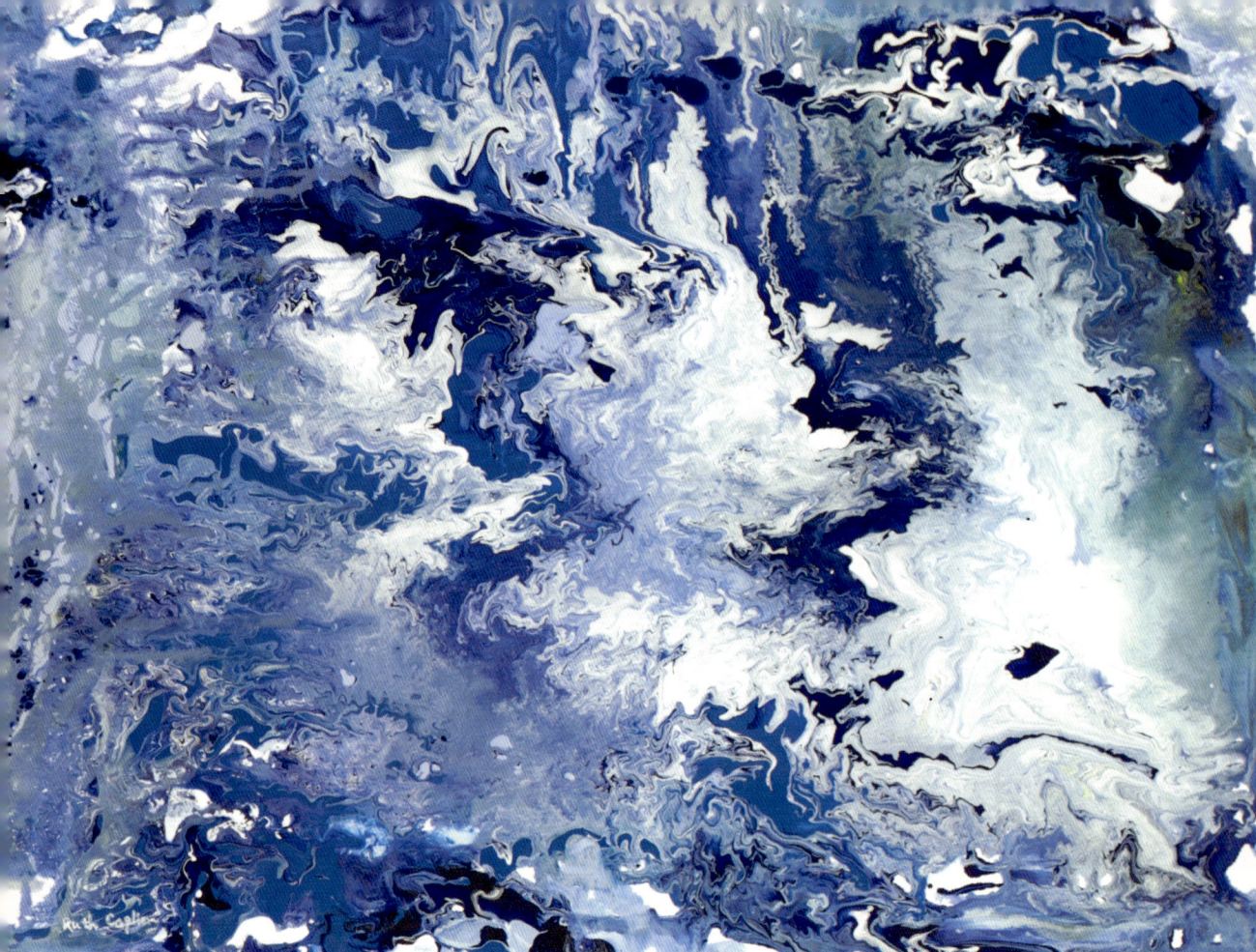

*Best Beginner in the Abstract or Experimental Category*

# Turbulence
*Ruth Caplin*

Acrylics

> After visiting local artist Peter Hicks in his studio and being inspired by his DVD, I wanted to try something free and flowing. Thus I started exploring the use of pouring fluid acrylic paints. Although *Turbulence* is nothing like Peter Hicks paintings, I enjoyed the experience of moving the paint in a totally different way from usual, blending colours and forming wave-like patterns. It was a satisfying encounter with a medium that was new to me.

# March/April

**31** Monday

**1** Tuesday

**2** Wednesday

**3** Thursday

**4** Friday

**5** Saturday

**6** Sunday

| APRIL | | | | | | |
|---|---|---|---|---|---|---|
| M | T | W | T | F | S | S |
|   | 1 | 2 | 3 | 4 | 5 | 6 |
| 7 | 8 | 9 | 10 | 11 | 12 | 13 |
| 14 | 15 | 16 | 17 | 18 | 19 | 20 |
| 21 | 22 | 23 | 24 | 25 | 26 | 27 |
| 28 | 29 | 30 | | | | |

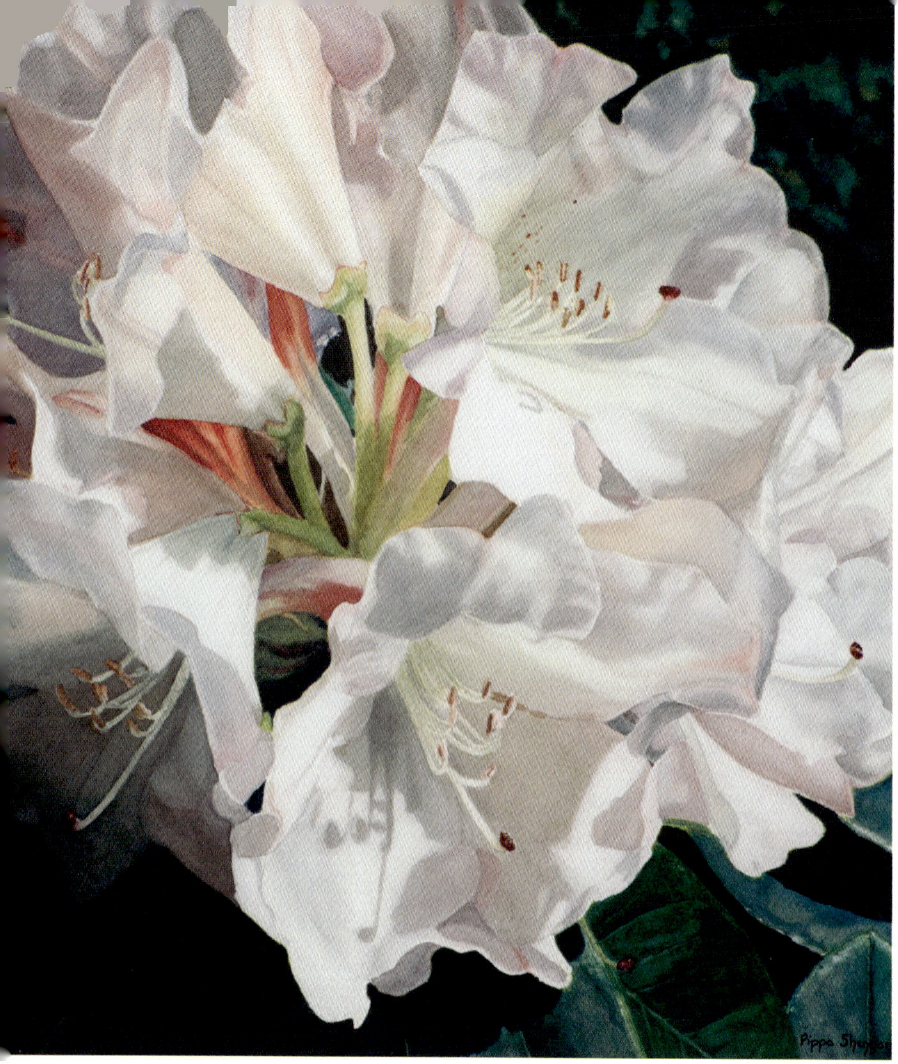

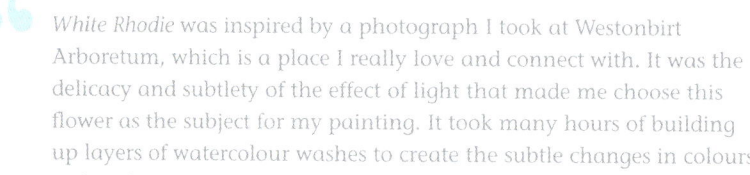

*Flowers or Gardens Category Winner*

# White Rhodie

*Pippa Shennan*

Watercolour

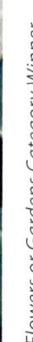

" *White Rhodie* was inspired by a photograph I took at Westonbirt Arboretum, which is a place I really love and connect with. It was the delicacy and subtlety of the effect of light that made me choose this flower as the subject for my painting. It took many hours of building up layers of watercolour washes to create the subtle changes in colours within the white petals. "

www.pippashennan.com

# April

7
Monday

8
Tuesday

9
Wednesday

10
Thursday

11
Friday

12
Saturday

13
Sunday

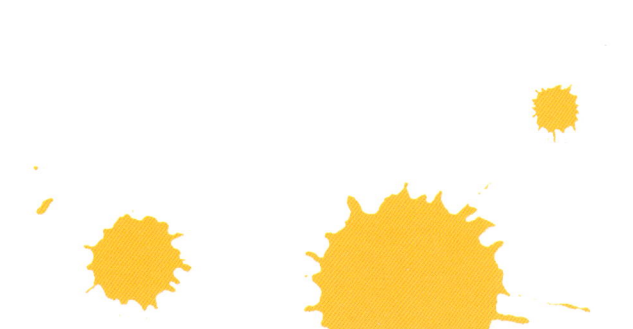

| APRIL | | | | | | |
|---|---|---|---|---|---|---|
| M | T | W | T | F | S | S |
|  | 1 | 2 | 3 | 4 | 5 | 6 |
| 7 | 8 | 9 | 10 | 11 | 12 | 13 |
| 14 | 15 | 16 | 17 | 18 | 19 | 20 |
| 21 | 22 | 23 | 24 | 25 | 26 | 27 |
| 28 | 29 | 30 | | | | |

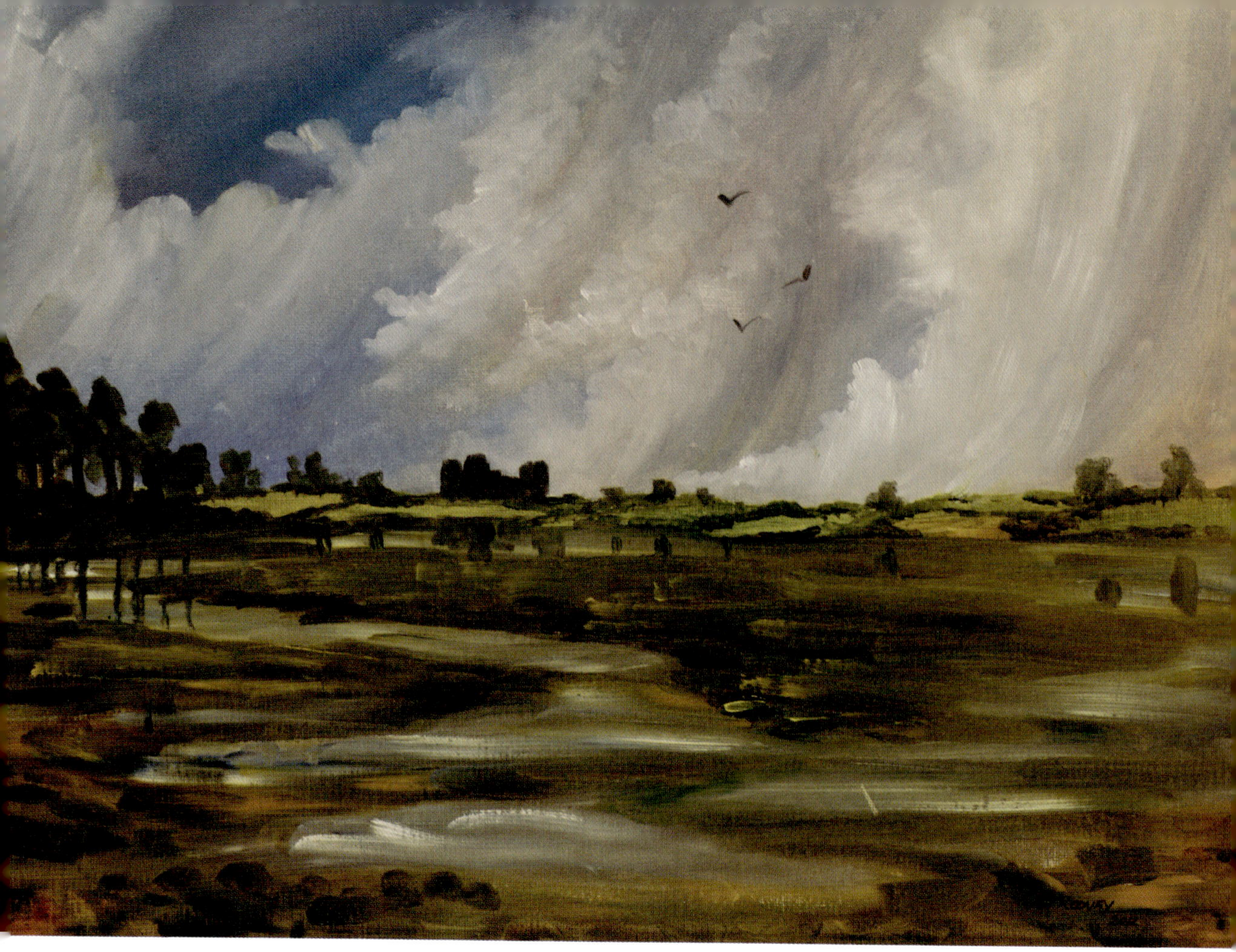

## Greencastle From Millbay
**Stephen Rooney**
*Oils*

*Best Young in the Landscape or Woodland Scene Category*

> I was out cycling and always take this route, which leads across the beautiful Carlingford Lough towards Greencastle and the roof of the thirteenth century Royal Castle there. It was a breezy day with heavy showers of thunder and rain nearby. I took a few photos, and came quickly home to paint the picture. I love this view and found it very easy to paint.

# April

## 14
Monday

## 15
Tuesday

## 16
Wednesday

## 17
Thursday

Good Friday (UK, Aus)
## 18
Friday

## 19
Saturday

Easter Sunday
## 20
Sunday

**APRIL**

| M | T | W | T | F | S | S |
|---|---|---|---|---|---|---|
|   | 1 | 2 | 3 | 4 | 5 | 6 |
| 7 | 8 | 9 | 10 | 11 | 12 | 13 |
| 14 | 15 | 16 | 17 | 18 | 19 | 20 |
| 21 | 22 | 23 | 24 | 25 | 26 | 27 |
| 28 | 29 | 30 |   |   |   |   |

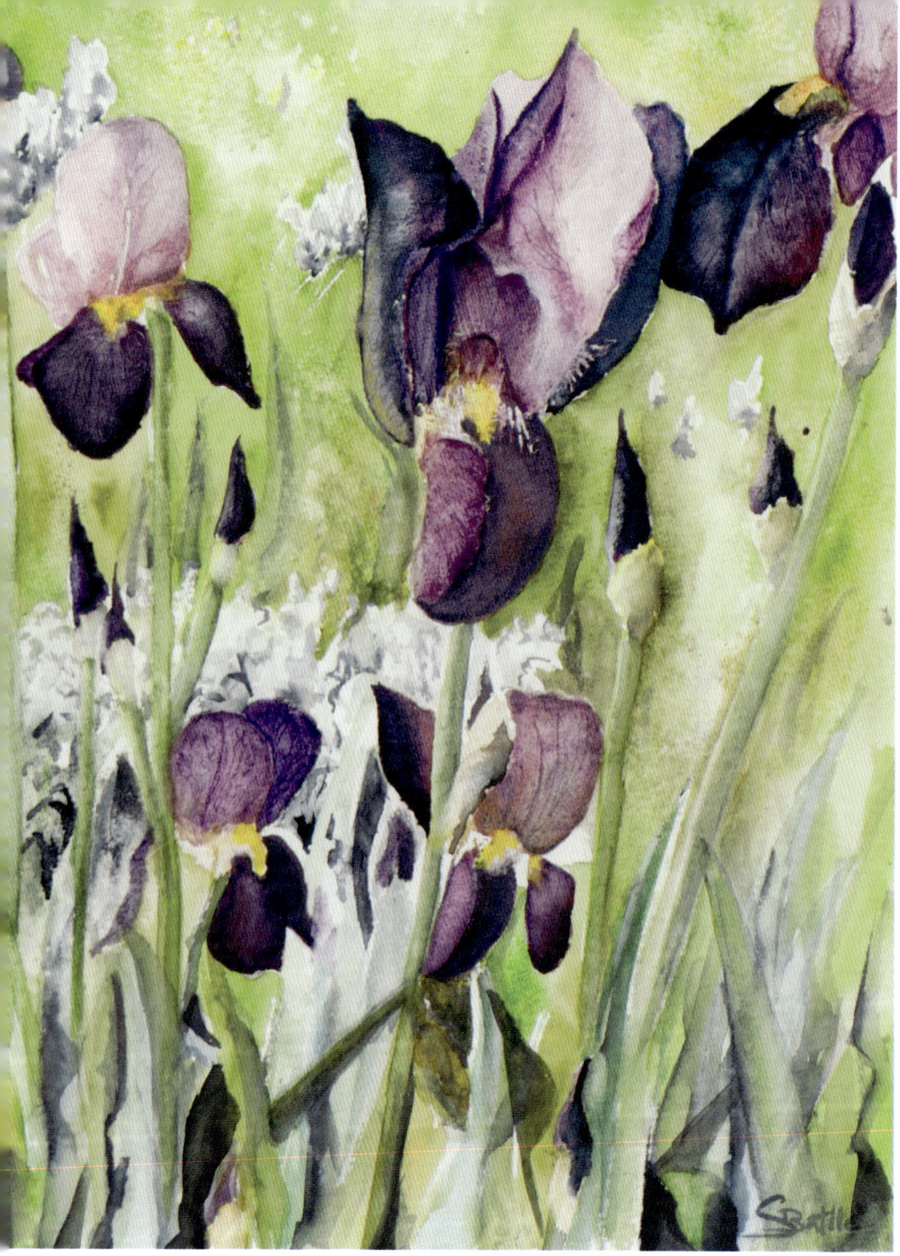

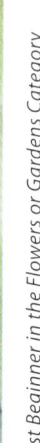

*Best Beginner in the Flowers or Gardens Category*

## April Irises

*Sylvie Batlle*

*Watercolour*

 While driving home, I suddenly noticed a most appealing bed of irises that made me feel compelled to stop. I grabbed my camera and took an unreasonable number of pictures; I adored those irises so much that painting them from these pictures felt irresistible. Passion took over my usual nervousness to start: before I realised, pigments in water started to flow and the irises began to come to life under my brushstrokes. A wonderful memory!

http://creatis.weebly.com

# April

*Easter Monday (UK, Aus)*

21 Monday

22 Tuesday

23 Wednesday

24 Thursday

25 Friday

26 Saturday

27 Sunday

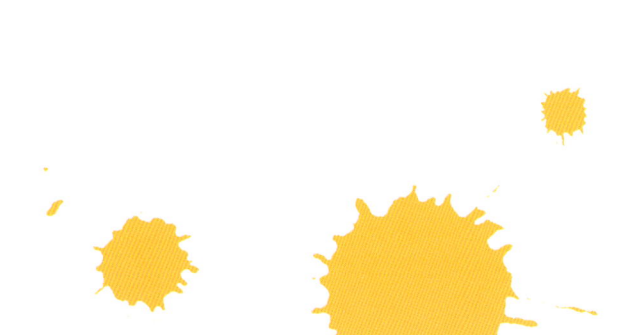

| APRIL | | | | | | |
|---|---|---|---|---|---|---|
| M | T | W | T | F | S | S |
|  | 1 | 2 | 3 | 4 | 5 | 6 |
| 7 | 8 | 9 | 10 | 11 | 12 | 13 |
| 14 | 15 | 16 | 17 | 18 | 19 | 20 |
| 21 | 22 | 23 | 24 | 25 | 26 | 27 |
| 28 | 29 | 30 | | | | |

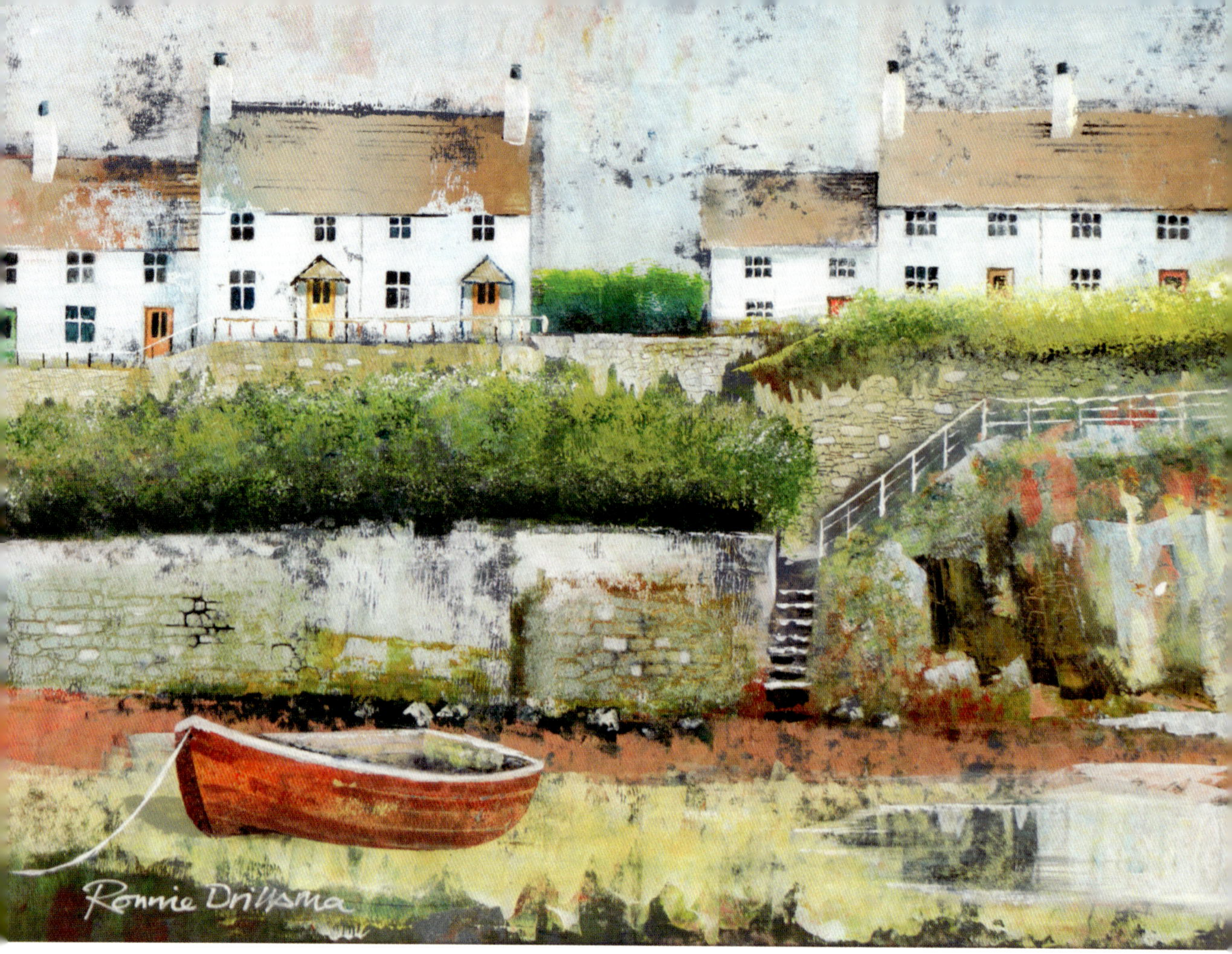

## Coastal Path, Anglesey
*Ronnie Drillsma*

Acrylics

*Highly Commended*

" This painting was created from sketches and photographs taken when my husband and I went to Anglesey for the day. I was in need of fresh inspiration, and the Isle has many beautiful beaches and coves, each one offering a painting. These little cottages are overlooking the sea, and they must have a wonderful view; for me, their white washed fronts and brightly painted doors nestled into the cliff top are just as lovely. "

www.ronniedrillsmaartgallery.vpweb.co.uk

# April/May

**28** Monday

**29** Tuesday

**30** Wednesday

**1** Thursday

**2** Friday

**3** Saturday

**4** Sunday

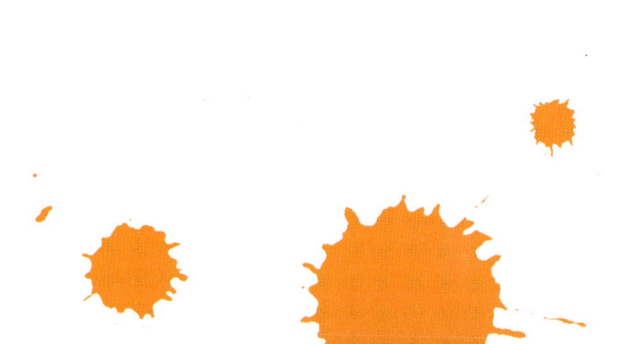

| | | | MAY | | | |
|---|---|---|---|---|---|---|
| M | T | W | T | F | S | S |
| | | | | 1 | 2 | 3 | 4 |
| 5 | 6 | 7 | 8 | 9 | 10 | 11 |
| 12 | 13 | 14 | 15 | 16 | 17 | 18 |
| 19 | 20 | 21 | 22 | 23 | 24 | 25 |
| 26 | 27 | 28 | 29 | 30 | 31 | |

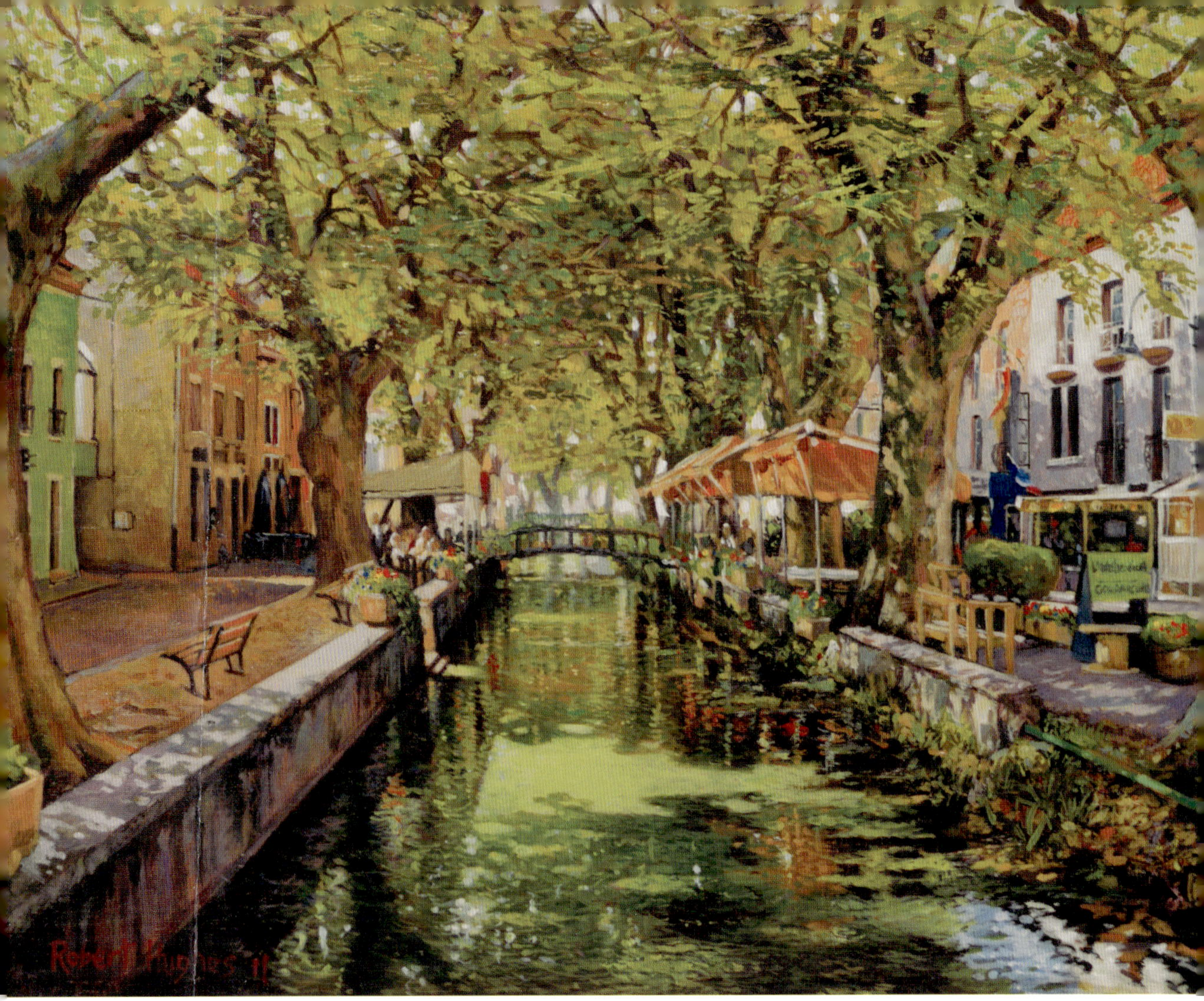

## Cafés On The Canal At Goudargues In France
*Robert Hughes*

Acrylics

*Highly Commended*

" I painted *Cafés On The Canal At Goudargues In France* from a photograph I downloaded from www.photos4artists.co.uk. When I saw the photograph I was taken by the perspective in the image, but more importantly by the reflections on the water. I could imagine any one of the Impressionists standing on the bridge and thinking 'I must paint this'. I thought it would be an interesting exercise to paint the image in an Impressionistic style. "

www.bobhughesartist.com

# May

*Bank Holiday (UK)*

**5** Monday

**6** Tuesday

**7** Wednesday

**8** Thursday

**9** Friday

**10** Saturday

*Mother's Day (US, Aus)*

**11** Sunday

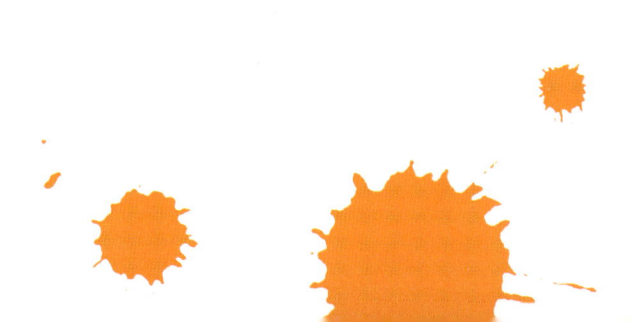

| MAY | | | | | | |
|---|---|---|---|---|---|---|
| M | T | W | T | F | S | S |
| | | | 1 | 2 | 3 | 4 |
| 5 | 6 | 7 | 8 | 9 | 10 | 11 |
| 12 | 13 | 14 | 15 | 16 | 17 | 18 |
| 19 | 20 | 21 | 22 | 23 | 24 | 25 |
| 26 | 27 | 28 | 29 | 30 | 31 | |

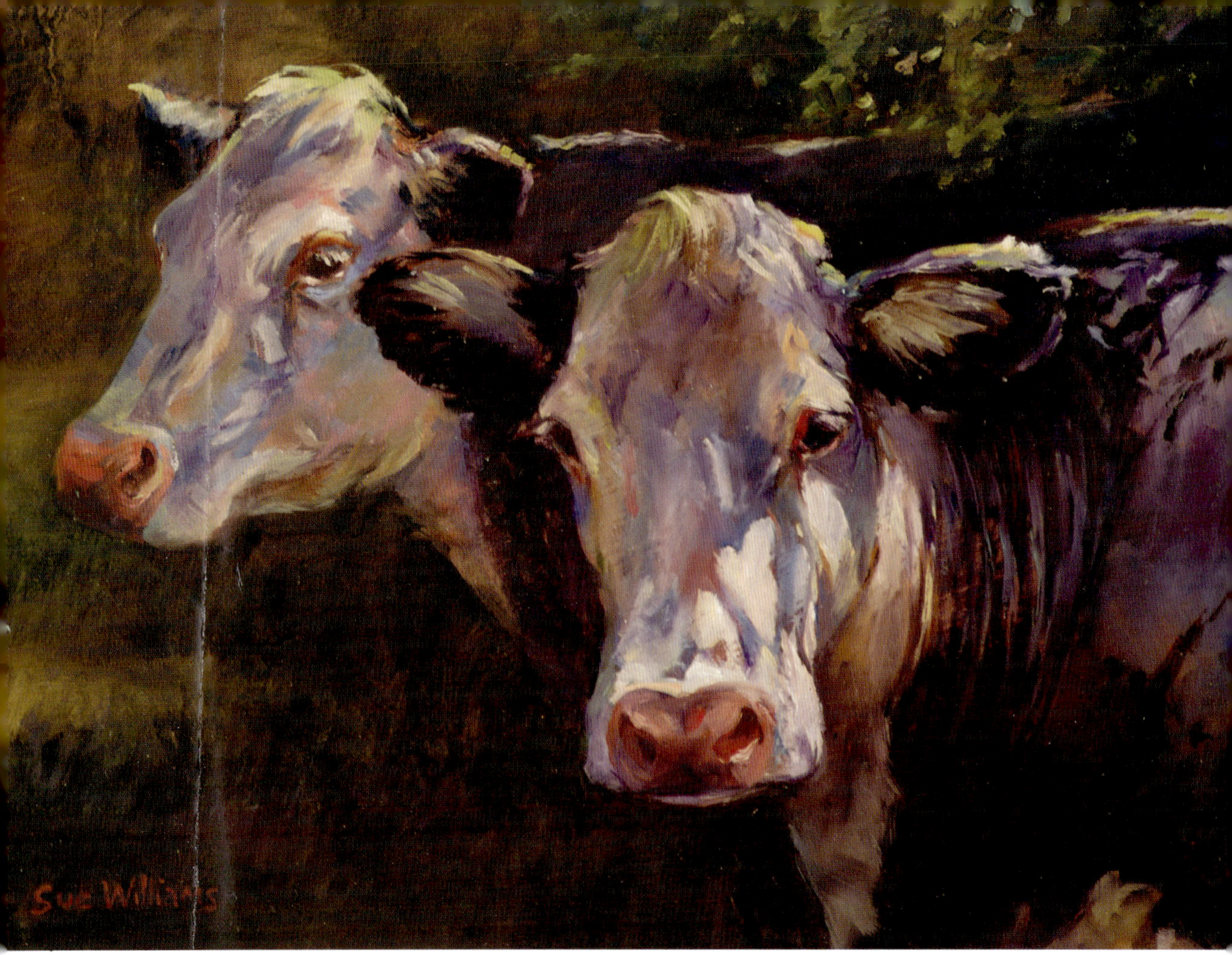

## Brown Eyed Girls
*Sue Williams*

Oils

Artist of the Year 2013

> *Brown Eyed Girls* was painted from my own photographs. I have been fortunate to take my painting classes at a local farm and painted the cows initially from life in watercolour. They doze in the shade on hot days and are elderly pets. I enjoy painting light and shadow, including all the amazing colours and reflected lights that are in shadows. I paint plein-air constantly, as nature is always so inspiring.

# May

### 12
Monday

### 13
Tuesday

### 14
Wednesday

### 15
Thursday

### 16
Friday

### 17
Saturday

### 18
Sunday

| MAY | | | | | | |
|---|---|---|---|---|---|---|
| M | T | W | T | F | S | S |
| | | | 1 | 2 | 3 | 4 |
| 5 | 6 | 7 | 8 | 9 | 10 | 11 |
| 12 | 13 | 14 | 15 | 16 | 17 | 18 |
| 19 | 20 | 21 | 22 | 23 | 24 | 25 |
| 26 | 27 | 28 | 29 | 30 | 31 | |

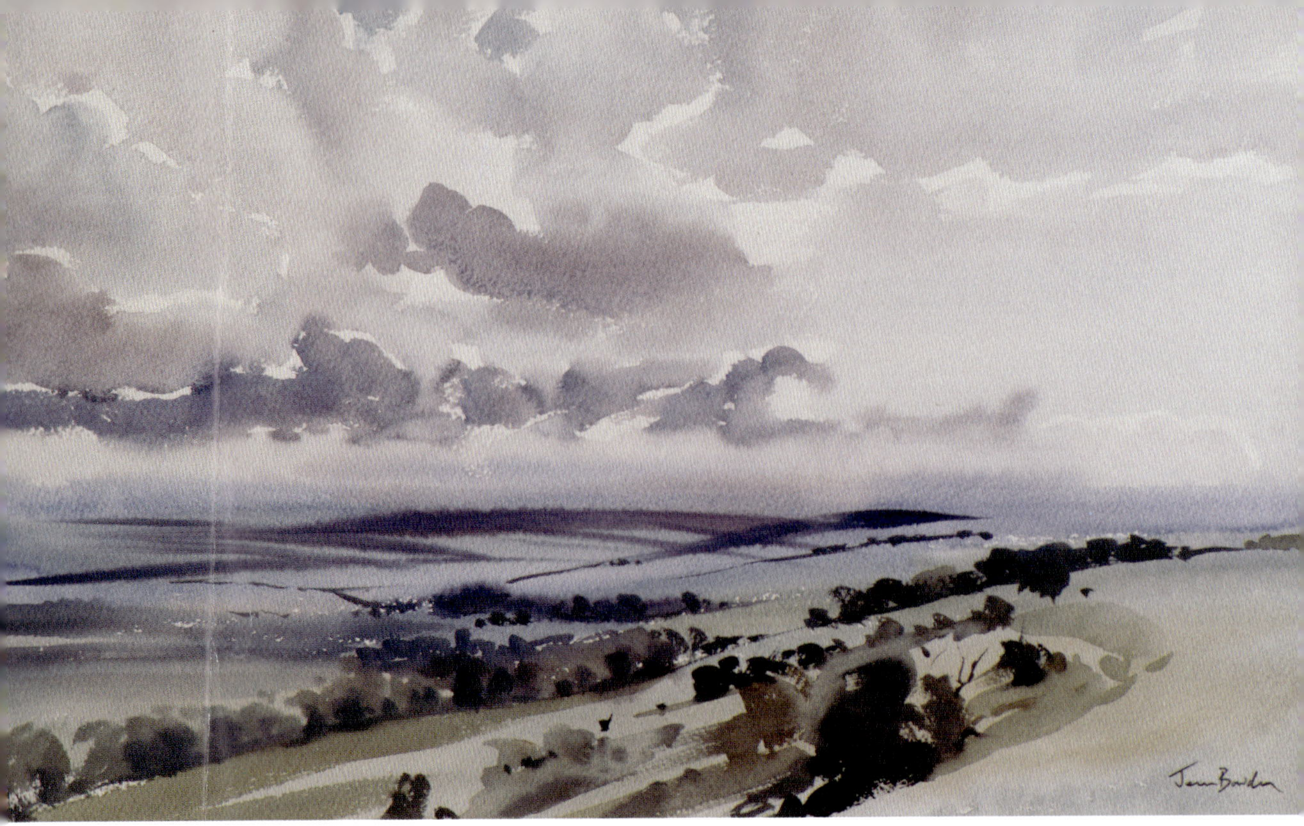

*Highly Commended*

## Across The Weald From Malling Down
*Jem Bowden*

*Watercolour*

 This was a 'flying by the seat of your pants' painting, as whilst I was at the scene there was a strong wind. It was done in a heady rush and a couple of washes, and I felt it captured something of my experience. I am normally more inspired to paint from life than from photos, but this was summer 2012! I was inspired by the grandeur of the view, which puts oneself into perspective.

www.jembowdenwatercolour.co.uk

# May

**19** Monday

**20** Tuesday

**21** Wednesday

**22** Thursday

**23** Friday

**24** Saturday

**25** Sunday

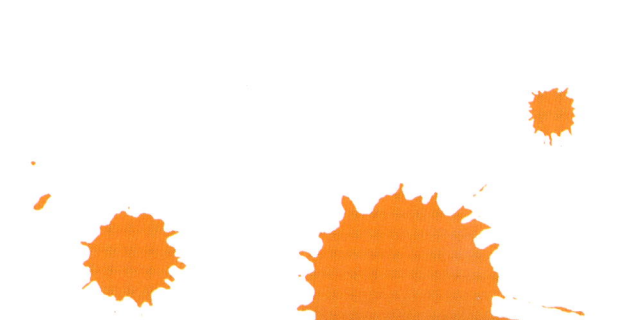

MAY

| M | T | W | T | F | S | S |
|---|---|---|---|---|---|---|
|   |   |   | 1 | 2 | 3 | 4 |
| 5 | 6 | 7 | 8 | 9 | 10 | 11 |
| 12 | 13 | 14 | 15 | 16 | 17 | 18 |
| 19 | 20 | 21 | 22 | 23 | 24 | 25 |
| 26 | 27 | 28 | 29 | 30 | 31 |   |

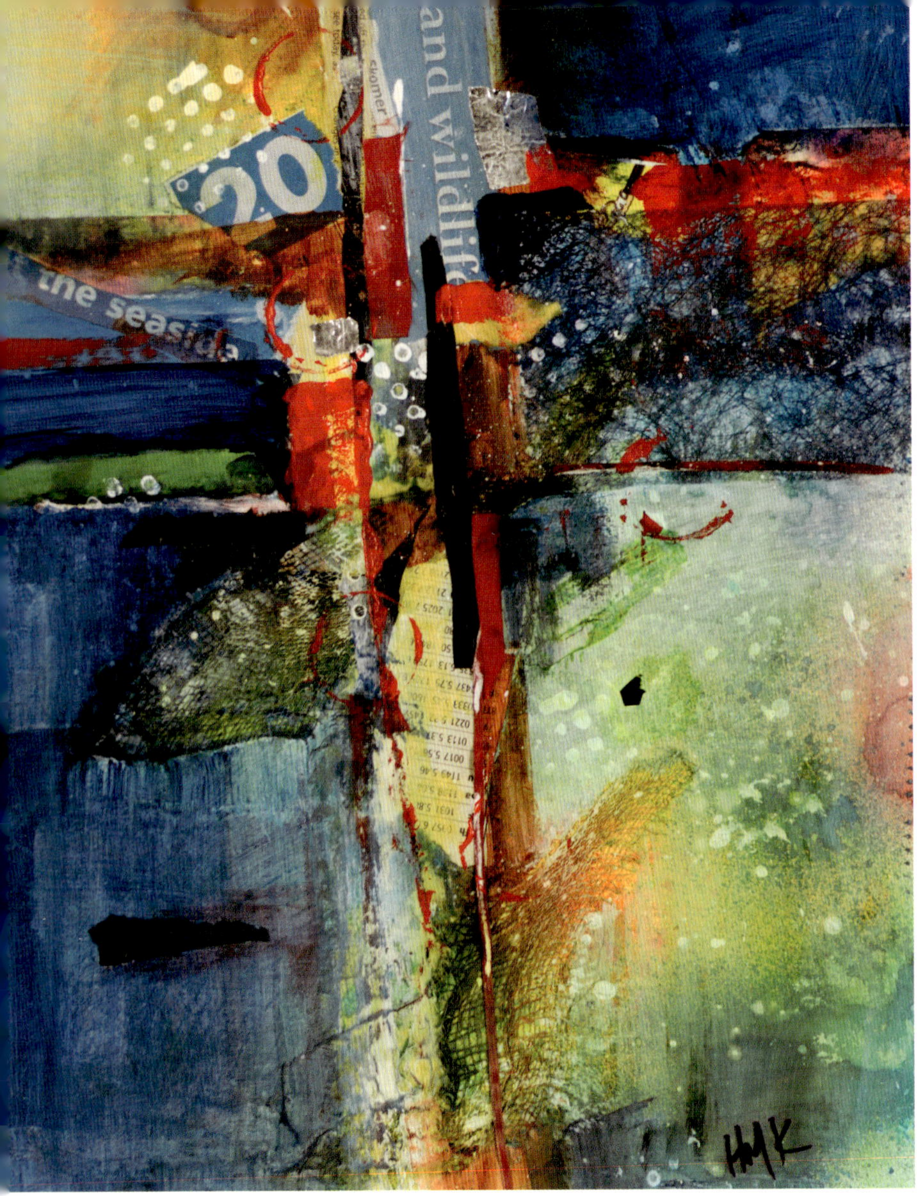

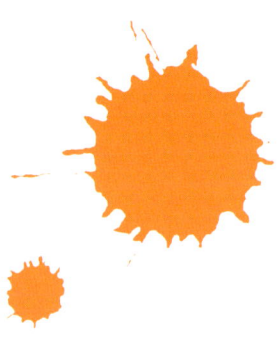

*Highly Commended*

## Across The Bay
*Helen Kaminksy*

Collage

" This painting was inspired by the beautiful, ethereal light of St Ives. Its origins were formed whilst sitting on the balcony of our holiday cottage overlooking the bay one evening, watching for seals – MAGIC! "

www.helenkaminsky.co.uk

# May/June

*Memorial Day (US)*
*Spring Bank Holiday (UK)*

**26** Monday

**27** Tuesday

**28** Wednesday

**29** Thursday

**30** Friday

**31** Saturday

**1** Sunday

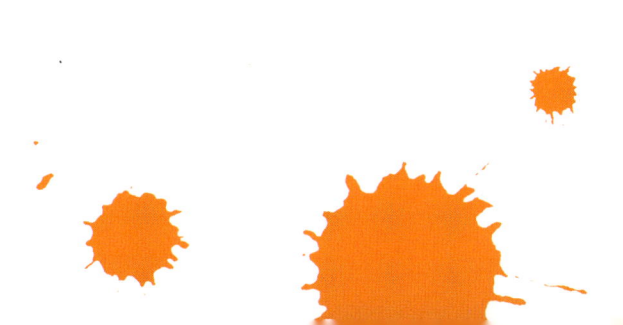

| MAY | | | | | | |
|---|---|---|---|---|---|---|
| M | T | W | T | F | S | S |
|  |  |  | 1 | 2 | 3 | 4 |
| 5 | 6 | 7 | 8 | 9 | 10 | 11 |
| 12 | 13 | 14 | 15 | 16 | 17 | 18 |
| 19 | 20 | 21 | 22 | 23 | 24 | 25 |
| 26 | 27 | 28 | 29 | 30 | 31 |  |

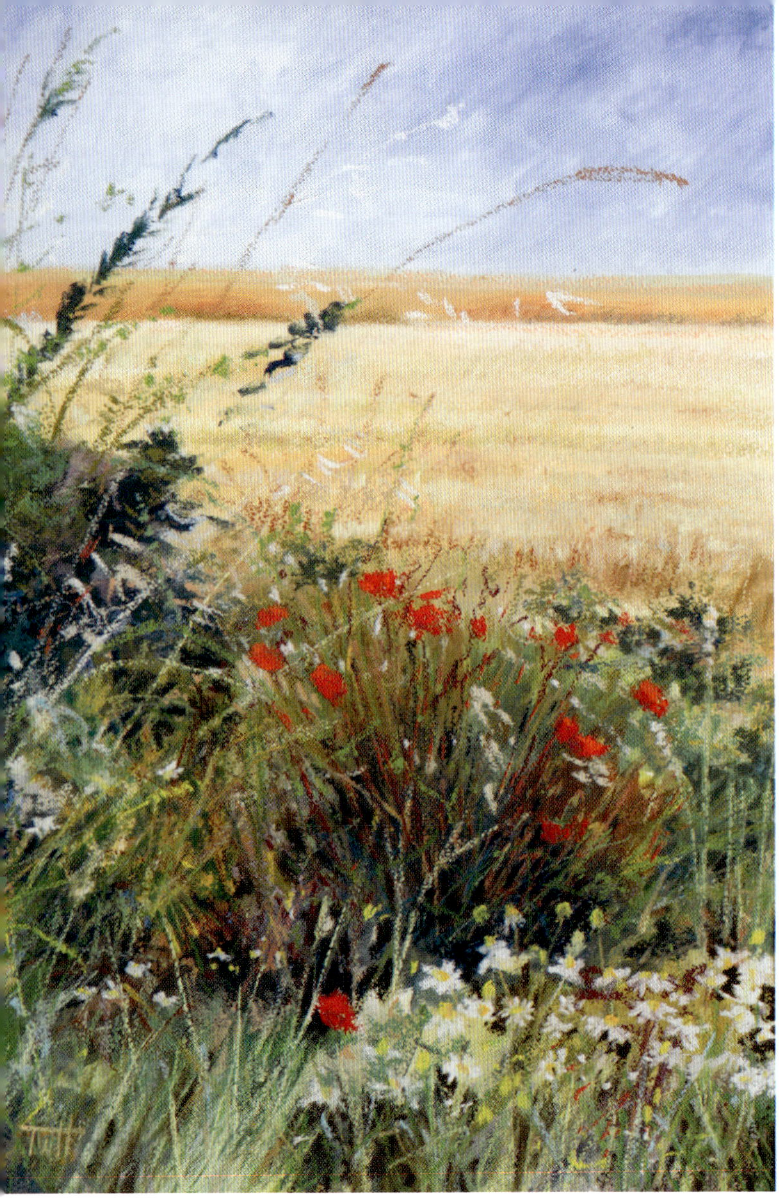

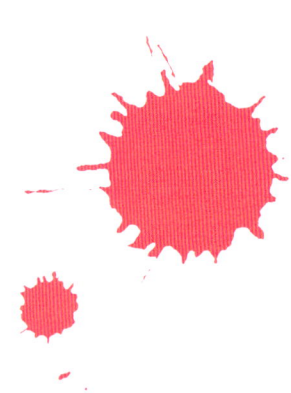

*Highly Commended*

## Summer Hedgerow

*Trevor Harwood*

Acrylics and Pastels

  This painting is a direct result of a demonstration undertaken last year. I was showing the differences between art surfaces and the way underpaintings can be developed. This picture started with some photos I had taken near Bicester of a hedgerow full of wild flowers. With an acrylic underpainting, building colour and layers, then a finish with Unison pastels, the art group have invited me back for a day workshop!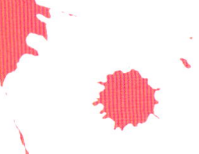

www.harwoodart.co.uk

# June

**2**
Monday

**3**
Tuesday

**4**
Wednesday

**5**
Thursday

**6**
Friday

**7**
Saturday

**8**
Sunday

| | | | JUNE | | | |
|---|---|---|---|---|---|---|
| M | T | W | T | F | S | S |
| | | | | | | 1 |
| 2 | 3 | 4 | 5 | 6 | 7 | 8 |
| 9 | 10 | 11 | 12 | 13 | 14 | 15 |
| 16 | 17 | 18 | 19 | 20 | 21 | 22 |
| 23 | 24 | 25 | 26 | 27 | 28 | 29 |
| 30 | | | | | | |

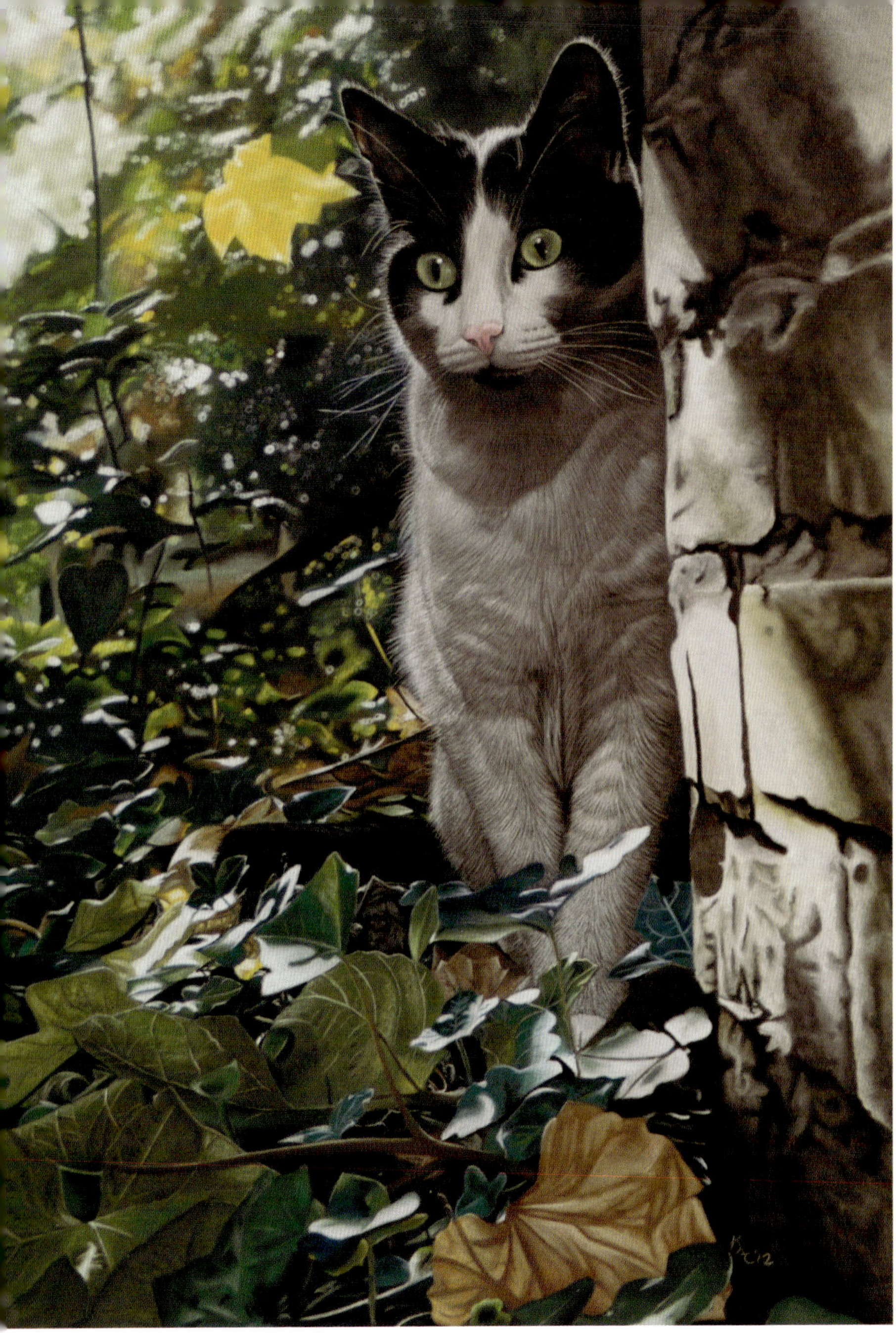

*Best Amateur in the Animal or Wildlife Category*

## On The Prowl
### Karie-Ann Cooper
*Pastels*

"*On The Prowl* is my first ever full pastel painting. I wanted to create a scene that can only be glimpsed through my artwork. This piece shows the hidden life of a cat, which we as owners are not often part of, but is their natural instinct and makes a cat what it is. I hope *On The Prowl* brings the secret nature of our feline companions to life."

www.artbykarie-ann.co.uk

# June

## 9
Monday

## 10
Tuesday

## 11
Wednesday

## 12
Thursday

## 13
Friday

## 14
Saturday

*Father's Day (US, UK)*

## 15
Sunday

| | | | JUNE | | | |
|---|---|---|---|---|---|---|
| M | T | W | T | F | S | S |
| | | | | | | 1 |
| 2 | 3 | 4 | 5 | 6 | 7 | 8 |
| 9 | 10 | 11 | 12 | 13 | 14 | 15 |
| 16 | 17 | 18 | 19 | 20 | 21 | 22 |
| 23 | 24 | 25 | 26 | 27 | 28 | 29 |
| 30 | | | | | | |

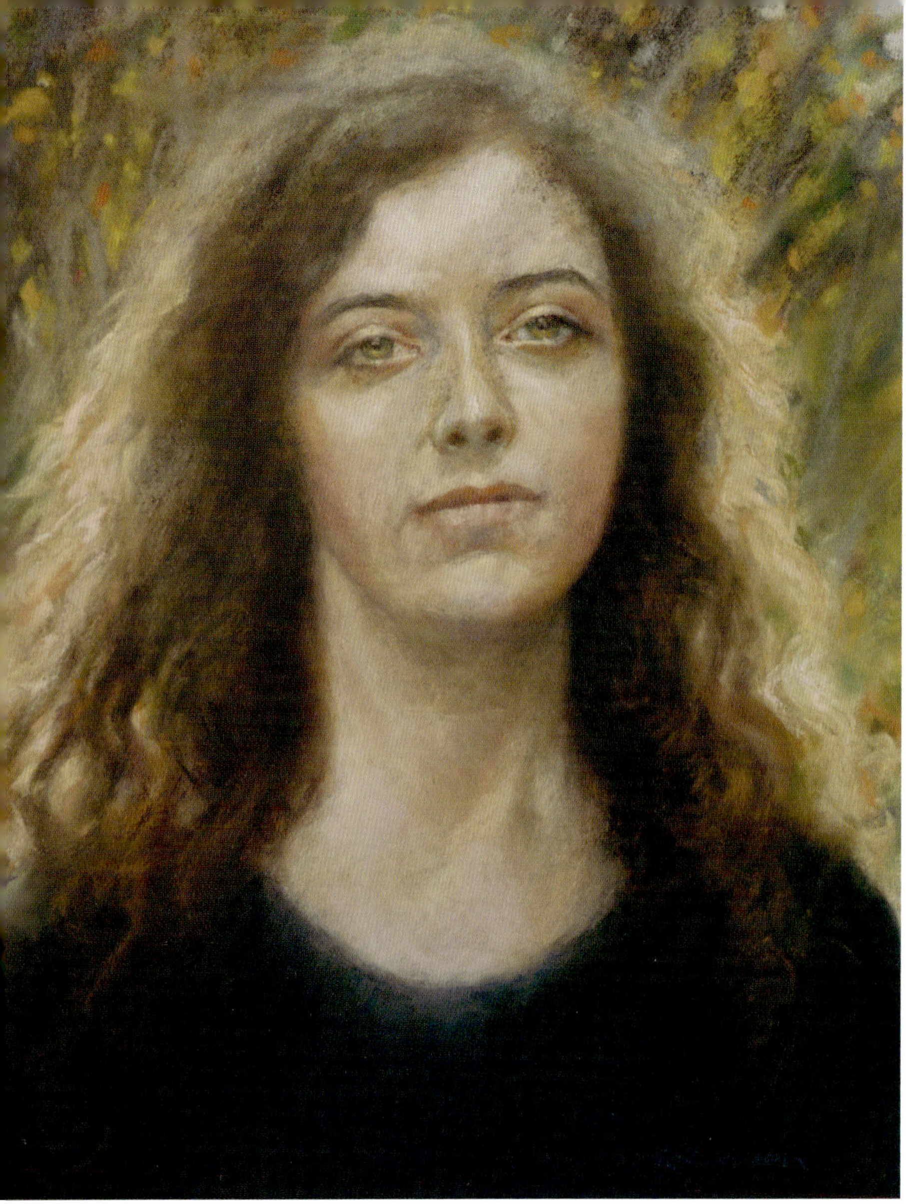

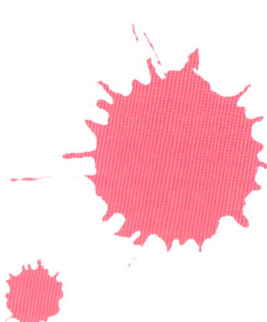

# Gloaming
*Margaret Ferguson*

*Pastels*

*Portrait or Figure Category Winner*

" This was painted after a perfect walk at dusk with my daughter. I loved the way the setting sun caught her hair and the leaves behind, giving a stained glass effect. In contrast, her skin tones were lit in soft pastel shades. "

www.margaretfergusonart.com

# June

## 16
Monday

## 17
Tuesday

## 18
Wednesday

## 19
Thursday

## 20
Friday

## 21
Saturday

## 22
Sunday

| JUNE | | | | | | |
|---|---|---|---|---|---|---|
| M | T | W | T | F | S | S |
|   |   |   |   |   |   | 1 |
| 2 | 3 | 4 | 5 | 6 | 7 | 8 |
| 9 | 10 | 11 | 12 | 13 | 14 | 15 |
| 16 | 17 | 18 | 19 | 20 | 21 | 22 |
| 23 | 24 | 25 | 26 | 27 | 28 | 29 |
| 30 | | | | | | |

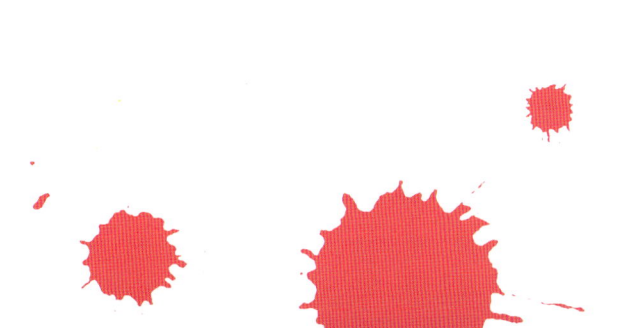

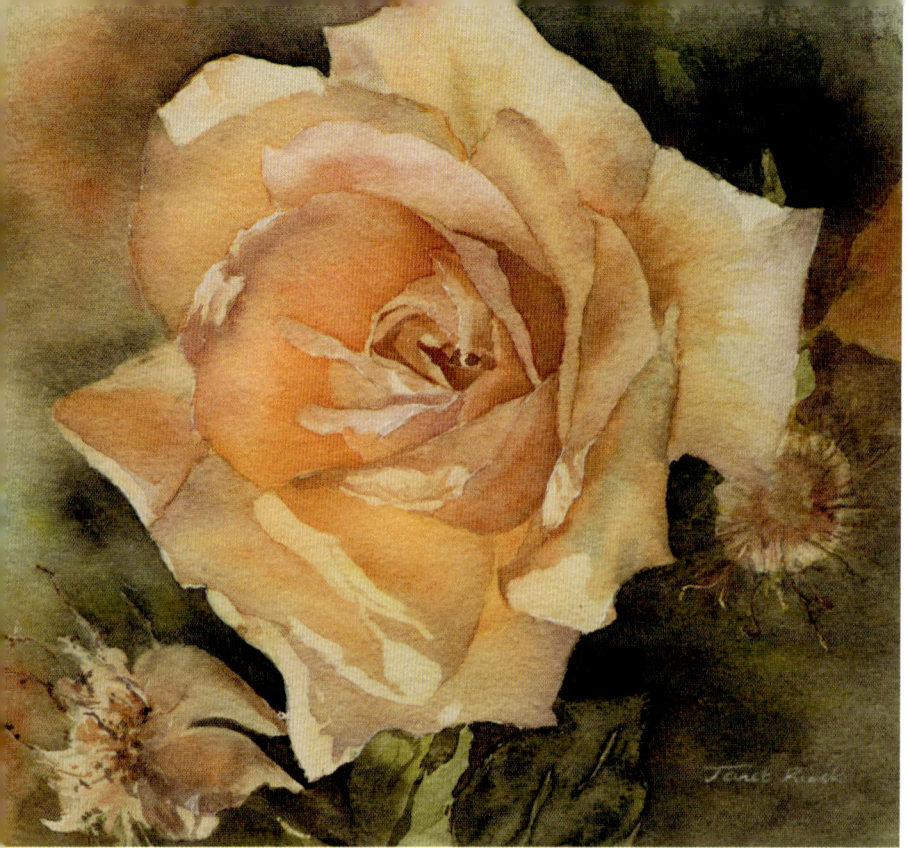

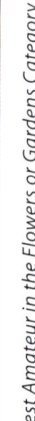

Best Amateur in the Flowers or Gardens Category

# My Garden's Bloom Of The Day
## *Janet Rusk*
*Watercolour*

" My kitchen window overlooks the garden. Often I glance out and spot fantastic light on a particular flower and rush to get my camera. This painting is all about colour, light and the delicacy of the rose. I looked very closely for colours on the rose and exaggerated them, using several layers of transparent watercolour. I recognise this rose from my garden, but hope I have enhanced and preserved it's beauty. "

# June

**23** Monday

**24** Tuesday

**25** Wednesday

**26** Thursday

**27** Friday

**28** Saturday

**29** Sunday

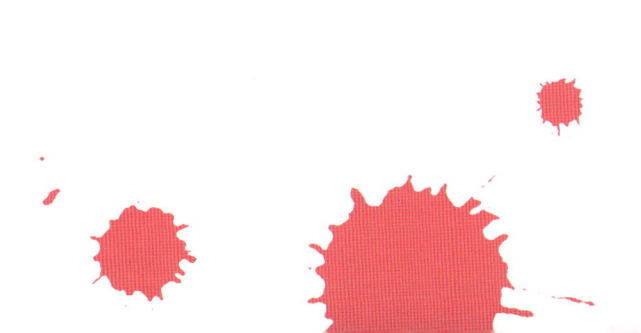

| JUNE | | | | | | |
|---|---|---|---|---|---|---|
| M | T | W | T | F | S | S |
|  |  |  |  |  |  | 1 |
| 2 | 3 | 4 | 5 | 6 | 7 | 8 |
| 9 | 10 | 11 | 12 | 13 | 14 | 15 |
| 16 | 17 | 18 | 19 | 20 | 21 | 22 |
| 23 | 24 | 25 | 26 | 27 | 28 | 29 |
| 30 | | | | | | |

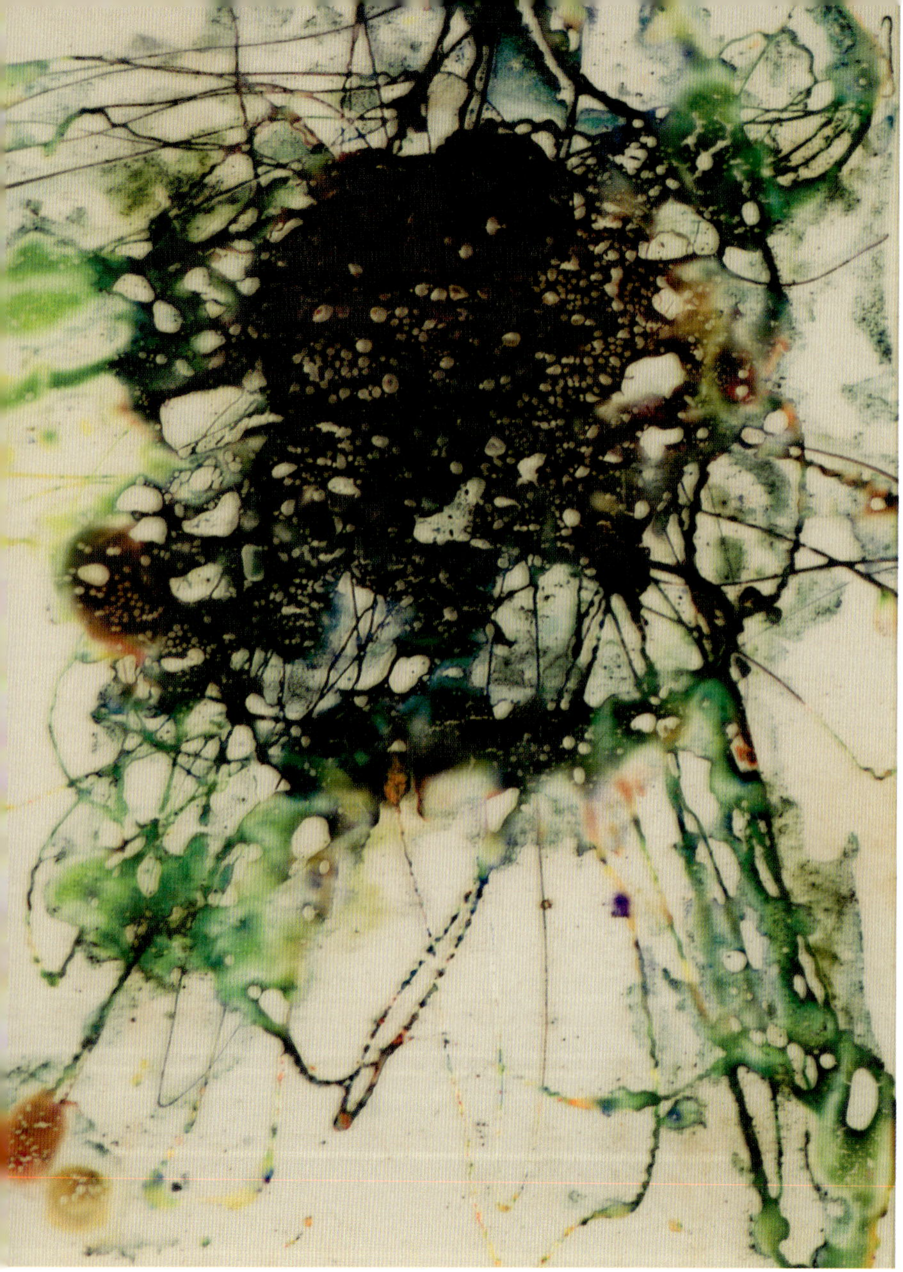

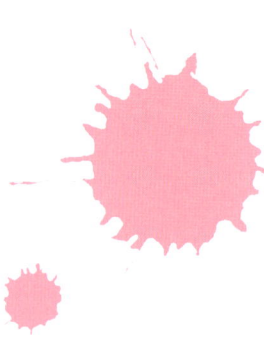

*Highly Commended*

# Diversity
*Kiana Soleimani*

*Mixed Media*

> I have been exploring the theme of close-ups, and have been particularly interested by the natural, harmonious patterns and colours evident in close-ups of the brain; neurons and their activity are fascinating. My piece was inspired by the artist Greg Dunn. I experimented with the materials and techniques: I used plastic, PVA glue, and Brusho inks, which is why I have submitted it into the Abstract and Experimental category.

# June/July

### 30
Monday

### 1
Tuesday

### 2
Wednesday

### 3
Thursday

*Independence Day (US)*

### 4
Friday

### 5
Saturday

### 6
Sunday

| **JULY** | | | | | | |
|---|---|---|---|---|---|---|
| M | T | W | T | F | S | S |
|   | 1 | 2 | 3 | 4 | 5 | 6 |
| 7 | 8 | 9 | 10 | 11 | 12 | 13 |
| 14 | 15 | 16 | 17 | 18 | 19 | 20 |
| 21 | 22 | 23 | 24 | 25 | 26 | 27 |
| 28 | 29 | 30 | 31 | | | |

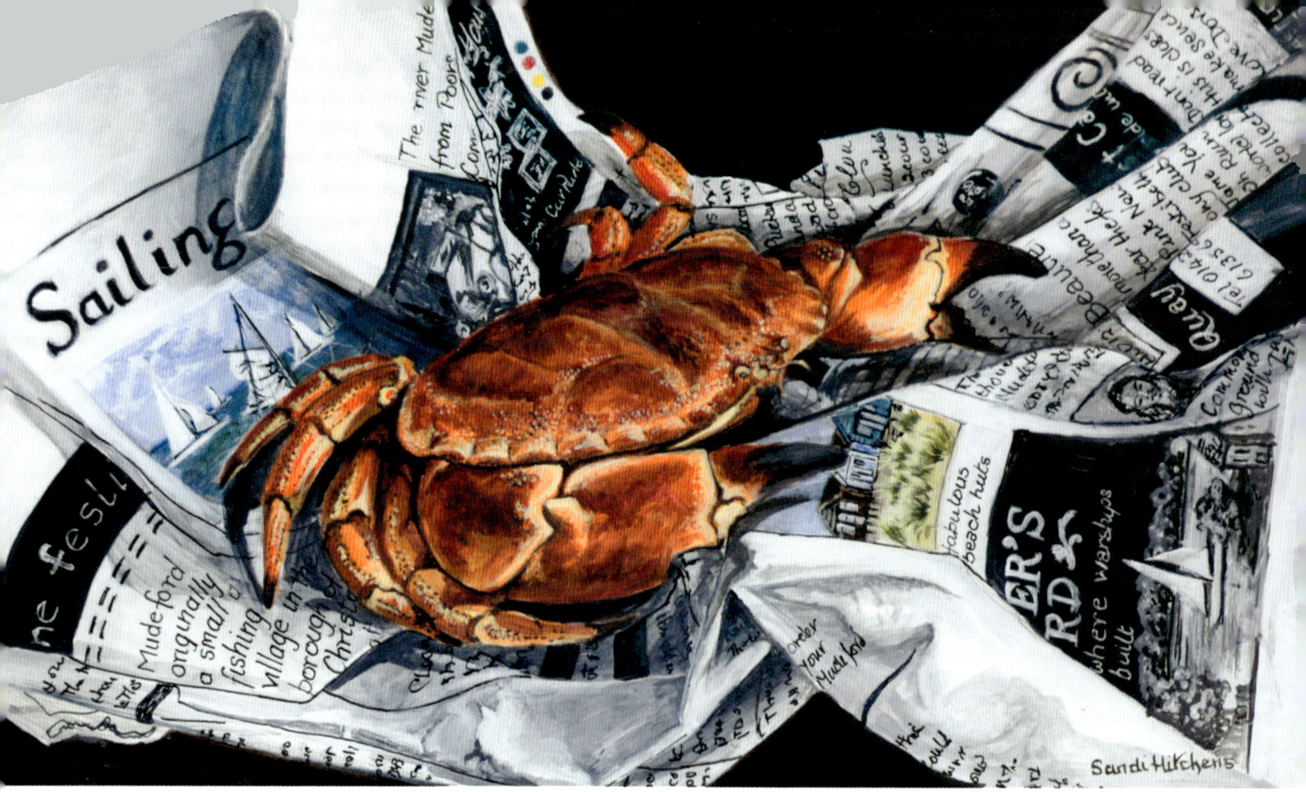

## Mudeford's Finest
### Sandi Hitchens
Acrylics

*Highly Commended*

> Mudeford in Dorset is known for its crab fishing, usually from the quay with bait and string. This was painted from life and was a progression of others I had done using newspaper. It was one of approximately 40 'foodie' pieces I had produced for a solo exhibition in Christchurch, to coincide with their Food and Wine Festival.

www.christchurchartsguild.org

# July

## 7
Monday

## 8
Tuesday

## 9
Wednesday

## 10
Thursday

## 11
Friday

## 12
Saturday

## 13
Sunday

| | | | JULY | | | |
|---|---|---|---|---|---|---|
| M | T | W | T | F | S | S |
| | 1 | 2 | 3 | 4 | 5 | 6 |
| 7 | 8 | 9 | 10 | 11 | 12 | 13 |
| 14 | 15 | 16 | 17 | 18 | 19 | 20 |
| 21 | 22 | 23 | 24 | 25 | 26 | 27 |
| 28 | 29 | 30 | 31 | | | |

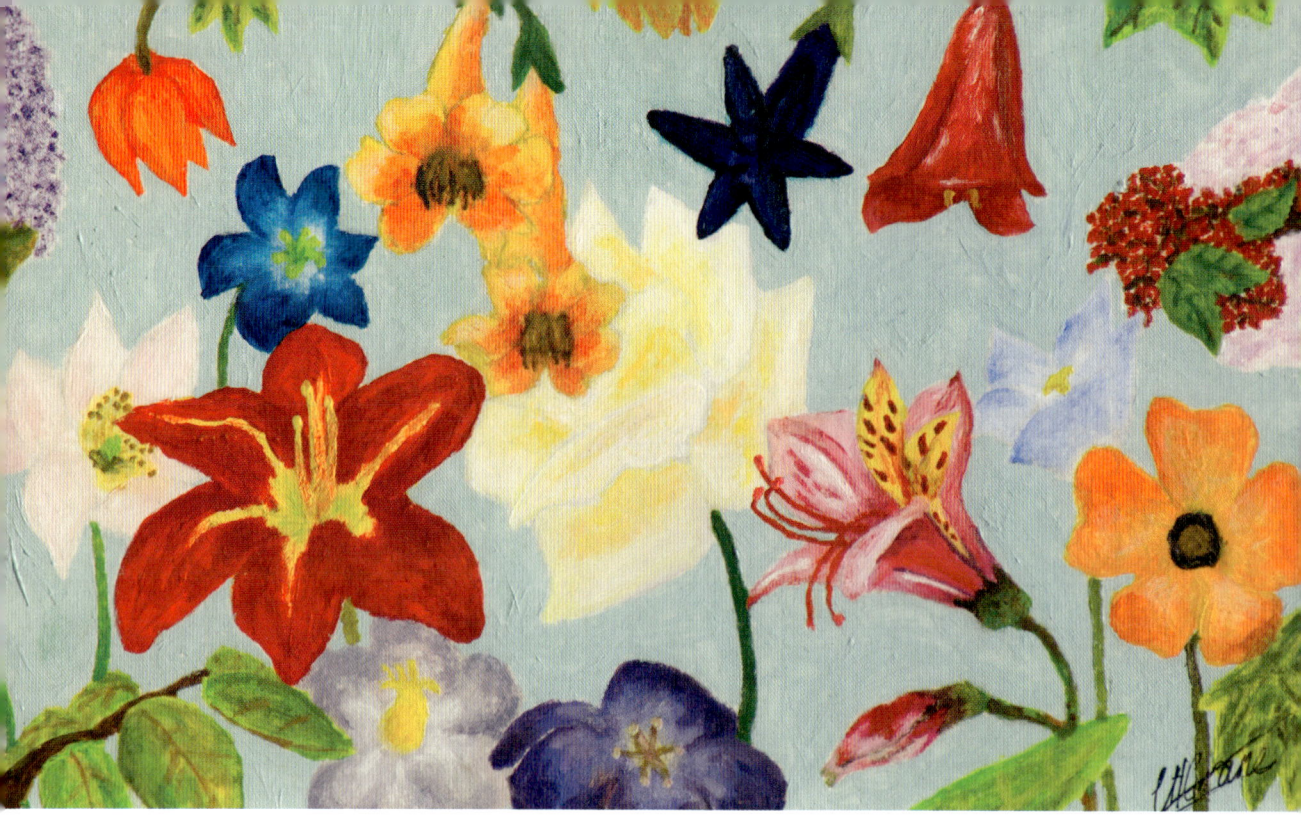

*Best Junior in the Flowers or Gardens Category*

# Flower Power
## Charlotte Crane
Acrylics

> I really enjoy painting flowers, and have done many paintings on this subject, ranging from tiny miniatures to quite large canvases. I find that flowers as a subject allows me to express my artistic creativity, as I love the bright colours and detail in them.

# July

## 14
Monday

## 15
Tuesday

## 16
Wednesday

## 17
Thursday

## 18
Friday

## 19
Saturday

## 20
Sunday

| | | | JULY | | | |
|---|---|---|---|---|---|---|
| M | T | W | T | F | S | S |
| | 1 | 2 | 3 | 4 | 5 | 6 |
| 7 | 8 | 9 | 10 | 11 | 12 | 13 |
| 14 | 15 | 16 | 17 | 18 | 19 | 20 |
| 21 | 22 | 23 | 24 | 25 | 26 | 27 |
| 28 | 29 | 30 | 31 | | | |

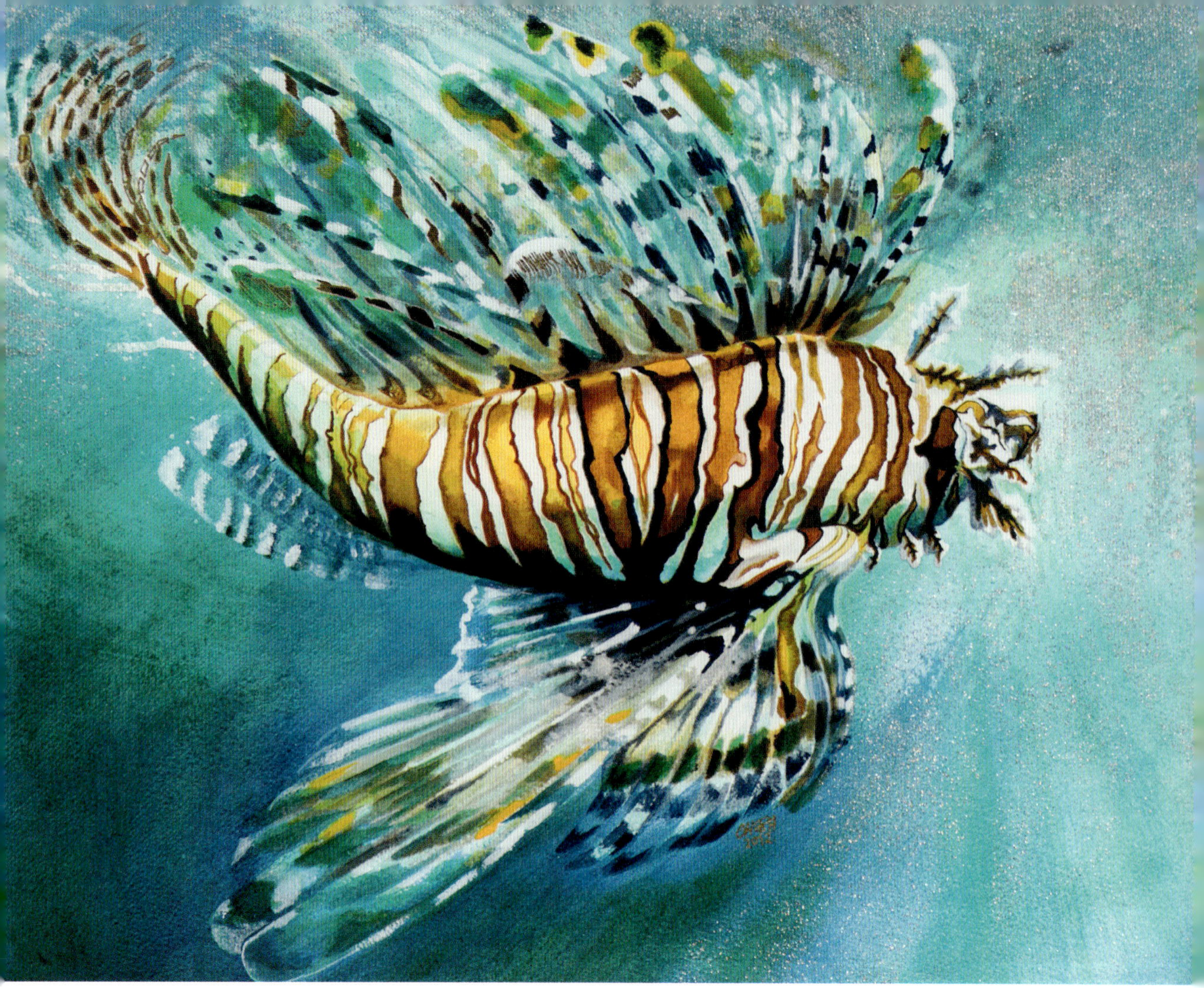

# Swish

## Christina Hopkinson

Mixed Media

*Highly Commended*

> Marine life has always fascinated me. Life underwater is, to us, as alien and hostile as being on the moon. We can dive, or visit aquariums, but we can never truly be a part of that world. *Swish* was inspired by a visit to an aquarium on holiday. I wanted to convey the feeling of being underwater, swimming with the lionfish, while the sunlight glimmered from above.

www.harmonyart.co.uk

# July

**21**
Monday

**22**
Tuesday

**23**
Wednesday

**24**
Thursday

**25**
Friday

**26**
Saturday

**27**
Sunday

| **JULY** | | | | | | |
|---|---|---|---|---|---|---|
| M | T | W | T | F | S | S |
|  | 1 | 2 | 3 | 4 | 5 | 6 |
| 7 | 8 | 9 | 10 | 11 | 12 | 13 |
| 14 | 15 | 16 | 17 | 18 | 19 | 20 |
| 21 | 22 | 23 | 24 | 25 | 26 | 27 |
| 28 | 29 | 30 | 31 |  |  |  |

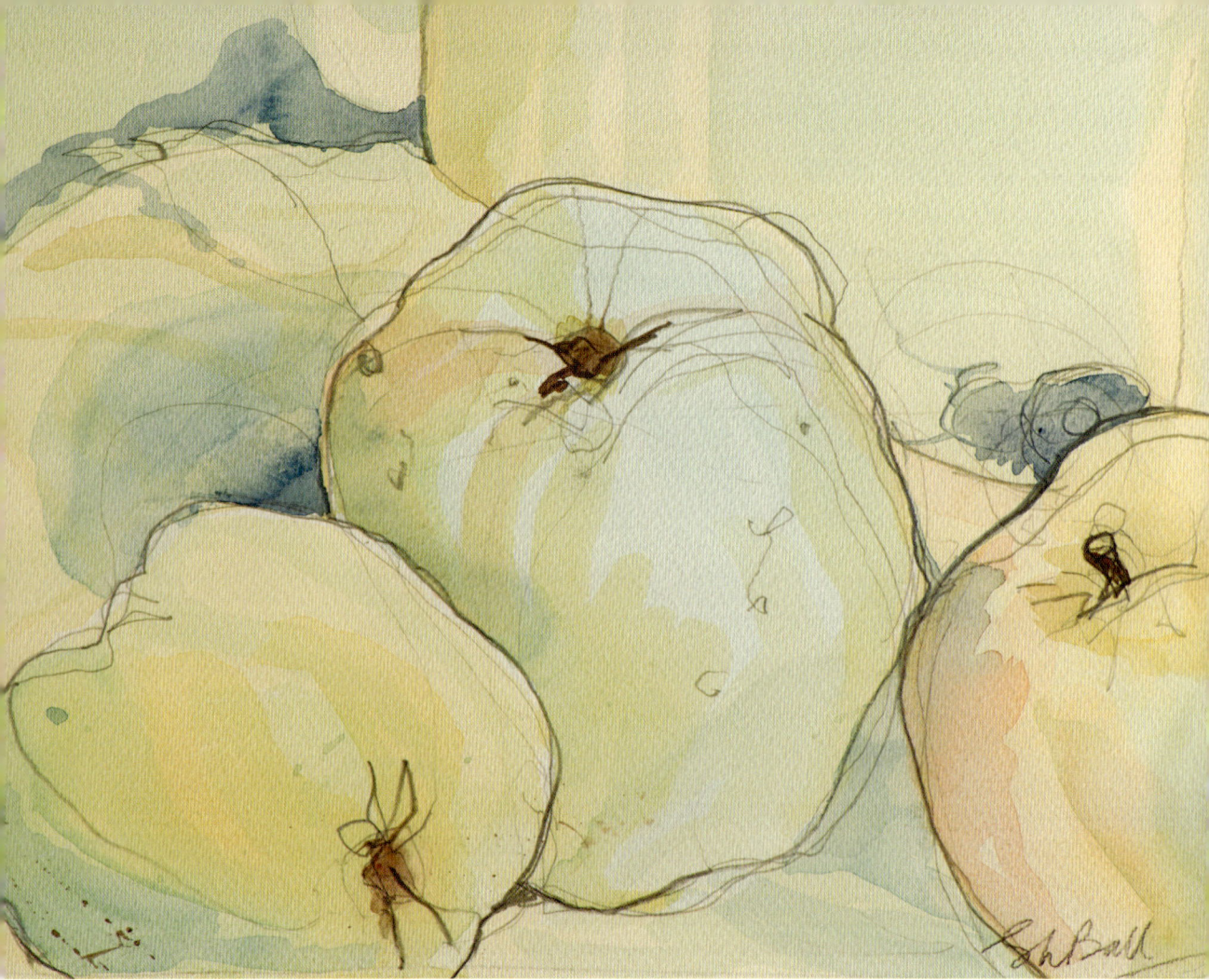

Still Life Category Winner

# Cooking Apples
*Sarah Ball*

Watercolour

> A mellow, misty early morning walk around the orchard in autumn reveals fresh dew-laden fruit with the morning sun upon them; immediately, I am captivated by their shape and colour. This old fashioned variety of apple, known as 'sheep's nose', has a particularly tantalising shape; I set about drawing the fruit to understand this. Composition is key. Placement is all. My intention is to convey the freshness of the fruit's beauty.

# July/August

**28** Monday

**29** Tuesday

**30** Wednesday

**31** Thursday

**1** Friday

**2** Saturday

**3** Sunday

| JULY | | | | | | |
|---|---|---|---|---|---|---|
| M | T | W | T | F | S | S |
|  | 1 | 2 | 3 | 4 | 5 | 6 |
| 7 | 8 | 9 | 10 | 11 | 12 | 13 |
| 14 | 15 | 16 | 17 | 18 | 19 | 20 |
| 21 | 22 | 23 | 24 | 25 | 26 | 27 |
| 28 | 29 | 30 | 31 | | | |

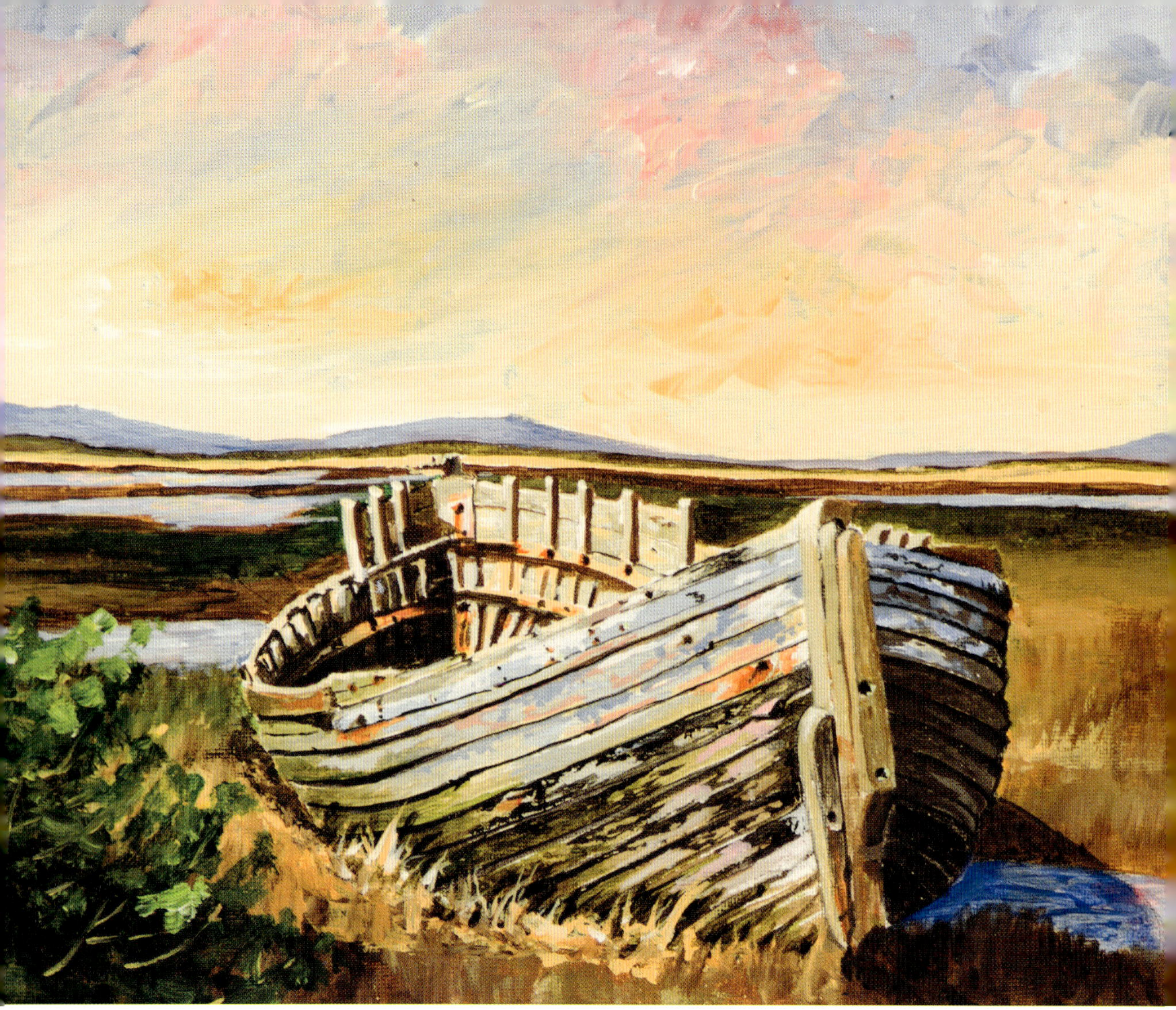

## Old Boat At Cley, Norfolk
*Hetty Essex*

Acrylics

Best Beginner in the Waterscape, Boats or Seascape Category

This derelict old boat has been the inspiration for many painters who wander along the path towards Blakeney Point near my home. I took a photograph as there was something special about the way in which the light caught the boat, and found that once I had rendered the shape of the boat to my satisfaction, the colours seemed to emerge without too much effort, and I surprised myself with the result.

# August

## 4
Monday

## 5
Tuesday

## 6
Wednesday

## 7
Thursday

## 8
Friday

## 9
Saturday

## 10
Sunday

| AUGUST | | | | | | |
|---|---|---|---|---|---|---|
| M | T | W | T | F | S | S |
| | | | | 1 | 2 | 3 |
| 4 | 5 | 6 | 7 | 8 | 9 | 10 |
| 11 | 12 | 13 | 14 | 15 | 16 | 17 |
| 18 | 19 | 20 | 21 | 22 | 23 | 24 |
| 25 | 26 | 27 | 28 | 29 | 30 | 31 |

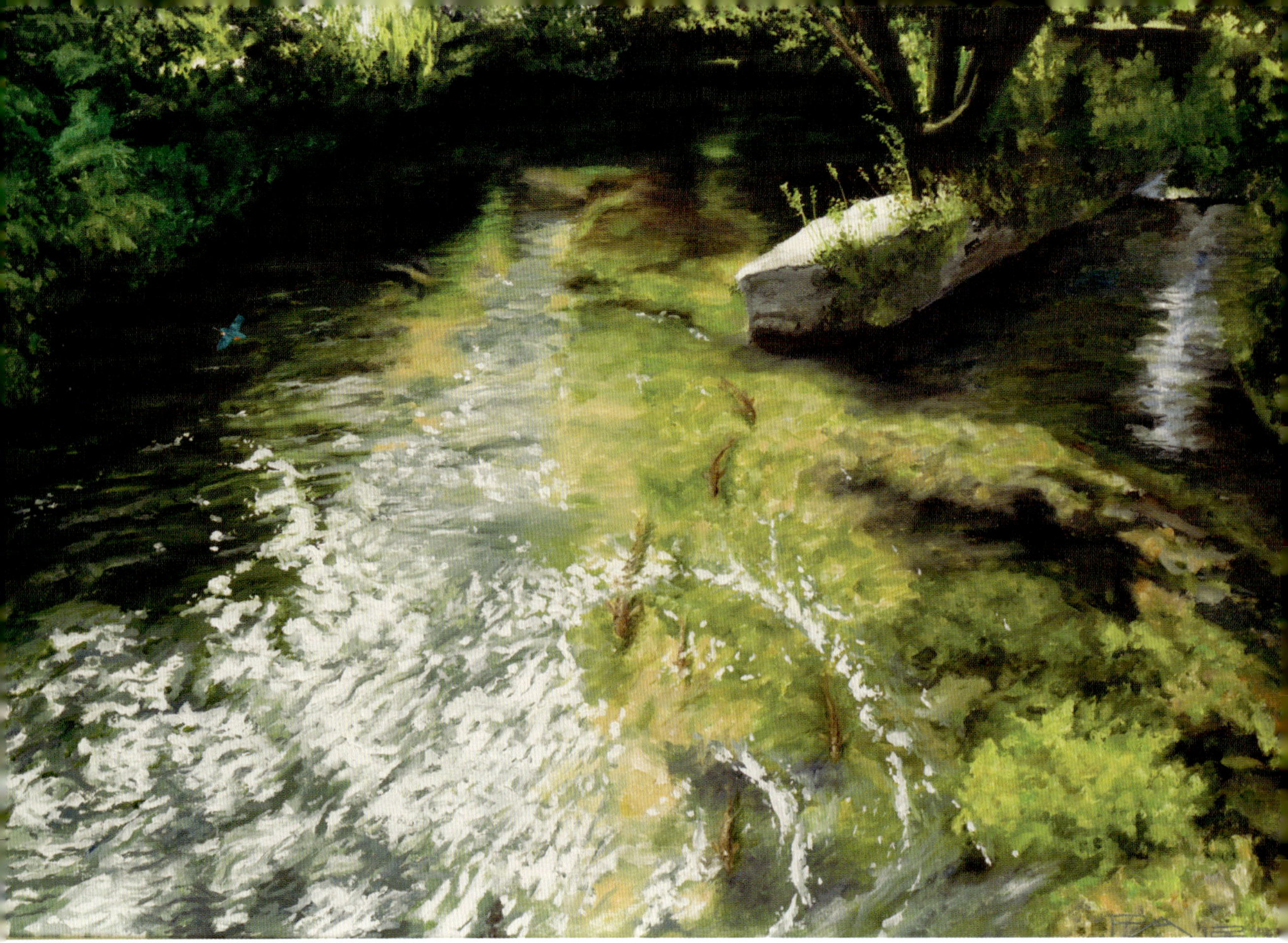

*Best Amateur in the Waterscape, Boats or Seascape Category*

## The Parting Of The Ways, The River At Motisfont

*Peter Arnold*

Oils

> This painting came about as a replacement. I entered a competition run by the National Trust at Motisfont called 'Open Water' and painted a picture for it along similar lines. I was very fortunate, as the painting got accepted and sold; my parents weren't so happy, as they had really wanted it. So I told them I would paint them a replacement and this is it. On the opening day of the exhibition at Motisfont I took a photo in the grounds, and that is what this painting is based on.

www.peterarnoldcreative.co.uk

# August

**11** Monday

**12** Tuesday

**13** Wednesday

**14** Thursday

**15** Friday

**16** Saturday

**17** Sunday

### AUGUST

| M | T | W | T | F | S | S |
|---|---|---|---|---|---|---|
|   |   |   |   | 1 | 2 | 3 |
| 4 | 5 | 6 | 7 | 8 | 9 | 10 |
| 11 | 12 | 13 | 14 | 15 | 16 | 17 |
| 18 | 19 | 20 | 21 | 22 | 23 | 24 |
| 25 | 26 | 27 | 28 | 29 | 30 | 31 |

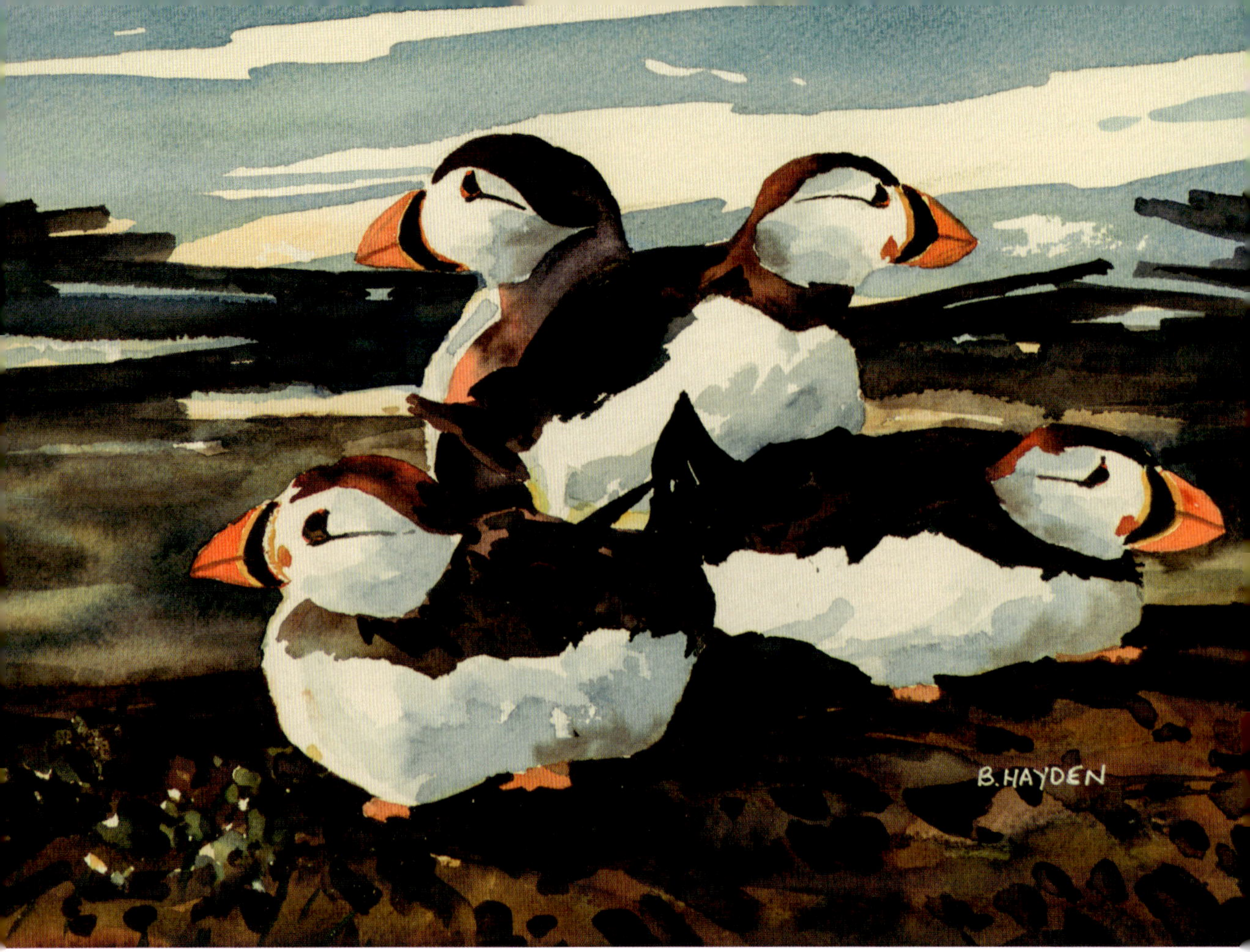

Wildlife or Animal Experimental Category Winner

# Squeezin' In
### Brigitte Hayden
Watercolour

> Who doesn't love puffins? I love their colours, their 'worried' expressions and their funny behaviour. I decided to create a group scene from my imagination. When I'd finished, one of the birds looked like it was having to squeeze into position, hence the title of the painting. It's a piece full of sunshine, colour and life; a great entry for the wildlife category, I thought.

www.minigallery.co.uk/Brigitte_Hayden

# August

**18**
Monday

**19**
Tuesday

**20**
Wednesday

**21**
Thursday

**22**
Friday

**23**
Saturday

**24**
Sunday

### AUGUST

| M | T | W | T | F | S | S |
|---|---|---|---|---|---|---|
|   |   |   |   | 1 | 2 | 3 |
| 4 | 5 | 6 | 7 | 8 | 9 | 10 |
| 11 | 12 | 13 | 14 | 15 | 16 | 17 |
| 18 | 19 | 20 | 21 | 22 | 23 | 24 |
| 25 | 26 | 27 | 28 | 29 | 30 | 31 |

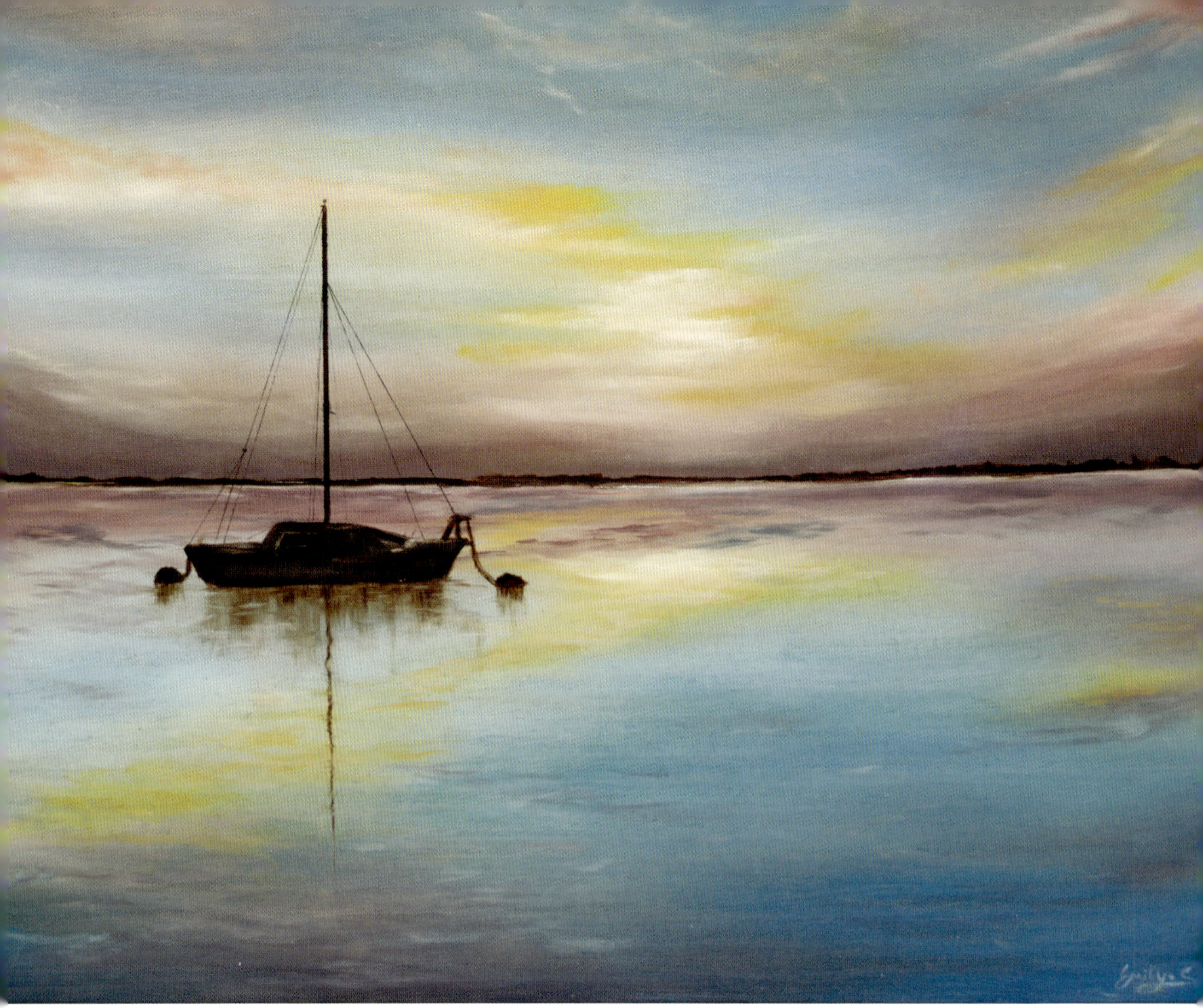

*Best Junior in the Waterscape, Boats or Seascape Category*

## Tranquillity

*Emily Speakman*

Oils

> My inspiration for painting *Tranquillity* was the colour in the sky that reflected on the sea to create a mirror image. The water is so still and silent it reminds me of times spent by the sea. I found painting the mast the most challenging aspect; making sure it was straight was quite nerve-wracking. I also spent quite some time on the reflections from the boat, as I wanted to show movement in the water.

www.emilyspeakmanart.co.uk

# August

*Summer Bank Holiday (UK)*

**25** Monday

**26** Tuesday

**27** Wednesday

**28** Thursday

**29** Friday

**30** Saturday

**31** Sunday

| AUGUST | | | | | | |
|---|---|---|---|---|---|---|
| M | T | W | T | F | S | S |
|  |  |  |  | 1 | 2 | 3 |
| 4 | 5 | 6 | 7 | 8 | 9 | 10 |
| 11 | 12 | 13 | 14 | 15 | 16 | 17 |
| 18 | 19 | 20 | 21 | 22 | 23 | 24 |
| 25 | 26 | 27 | 28 | 29 | 30 | 31 |

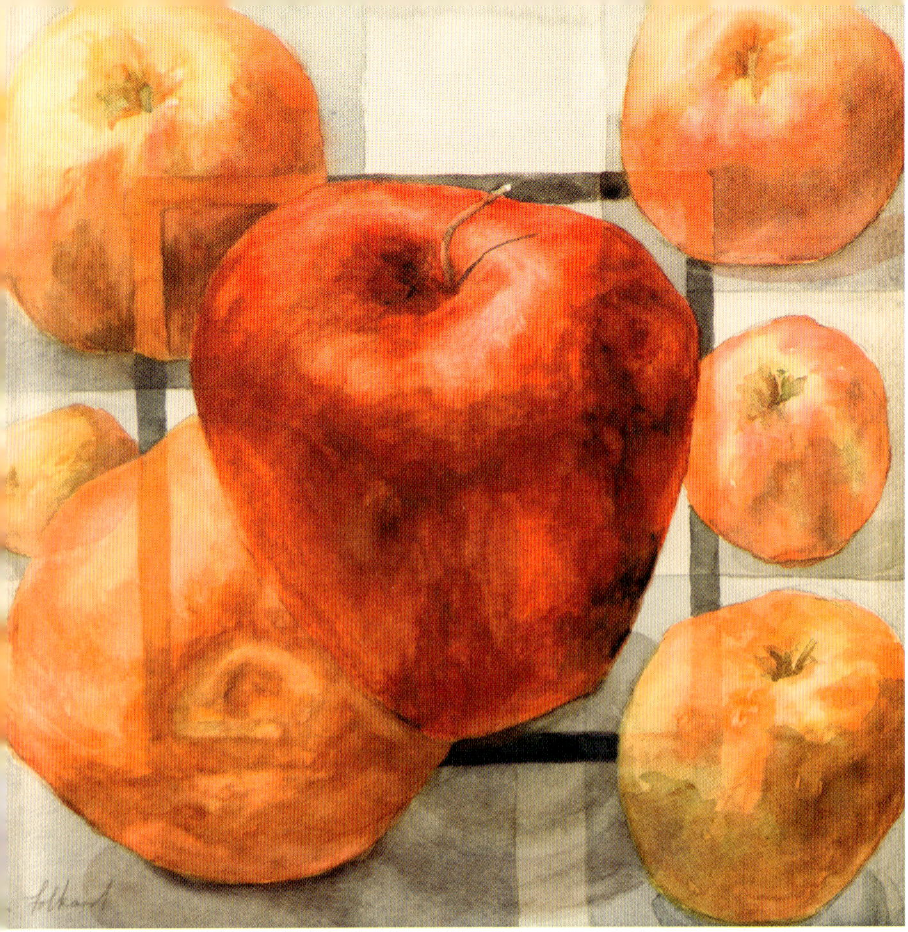

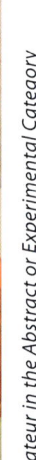

*Best Amateur in the Abstract or Experimental Category*

## One A Day...
*Lois Folkard*

Watercolour

*One A Day...* was painted from observational studies of apples in my fruit bowl at home. I like the square format for painting an apple, but wanted a different approach. Thinking about the saying 'An apple a day keeps the doctor away', I challenged myself to paint seven apples in seven squares. The most difficult decision was how to keep each apple and its square distinctive, yet blend the apples to make one picture.

www.loiszart.tripod.co.uk

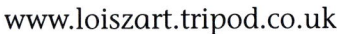

# September

*Labor Day (US)*

1
Monday

2
Tuesday

3
Wednesday

4
Thursday

5
Friday

6
Saturday

*Father's Day (Aus)*

7
Sunday

| | | SEPTEMBER | | | | |
|---|---|---|---|---|---|---|
| M | T | W | T | F | S | S |
| 1 | 2 | 3 | 4 | 5 | 6 | 7 |
| 8 | 9 | 10 | 11 | 12 | 13 | 14 |
| 15 | 16 | 17 | 18 | 19 | 20 | 21 |
| 22 | 23 | 24 | 25 | 26 | 27 | 28 |
| 29 | 30 | | | | | |

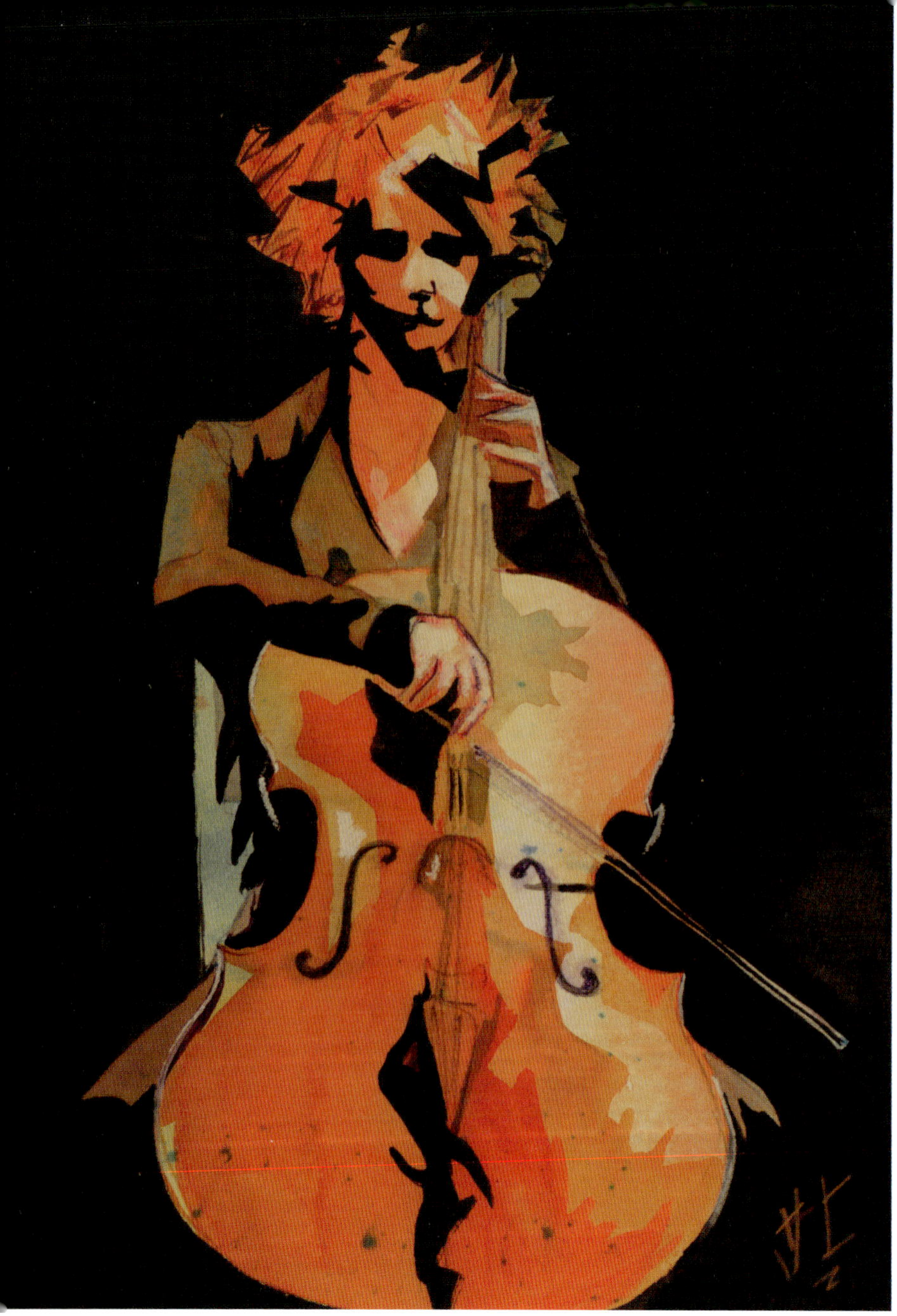

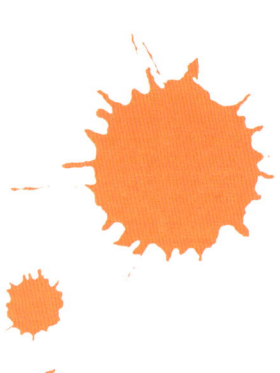

*Abstract or Experimental Category Winner*

# Cellist
*Julie Cross*

*Acrylic Inks, Watercolour and Watercolour Pencils*

*Cellist* is part of a recent series of figures, in which I have been experimenting with solid black acrylic ink, juxtaposed against transparent watercolour. An added wackiness is provided by the scribbled watercolour pencil used to make the drawing, and dramatic shadows from the stage lighting made abstracting the figure easier, too.

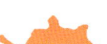

# September

**8** Monday

**9** Tuesday

**10** Wednesday

**11** Thursday

**12** Friday

**13** Saturday

**14** Sunday

### SEPTEMBER

| M | T | W | T | F | S | S |
|---|---|---|---|---|---|---|
| 1 | 2 | 3 | 4 | 5 | 6 | 7 |
| 8 | 9 | 10 | 11 | 12 | 13 | 14 |
| 15 | 16 | 17 | 18 | 19 | 20 | 21 |
| 22 | 23 | 24 | 25 | 26 | 27 | 28 |
| 29 | 30 | | | | | |

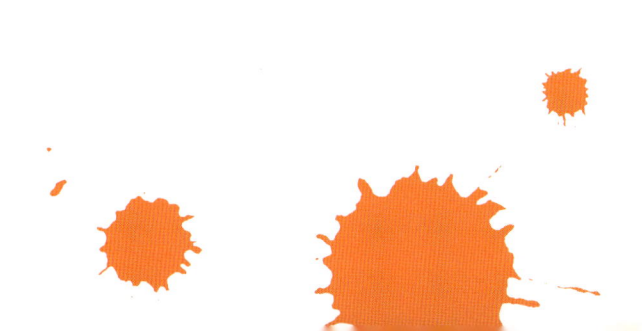

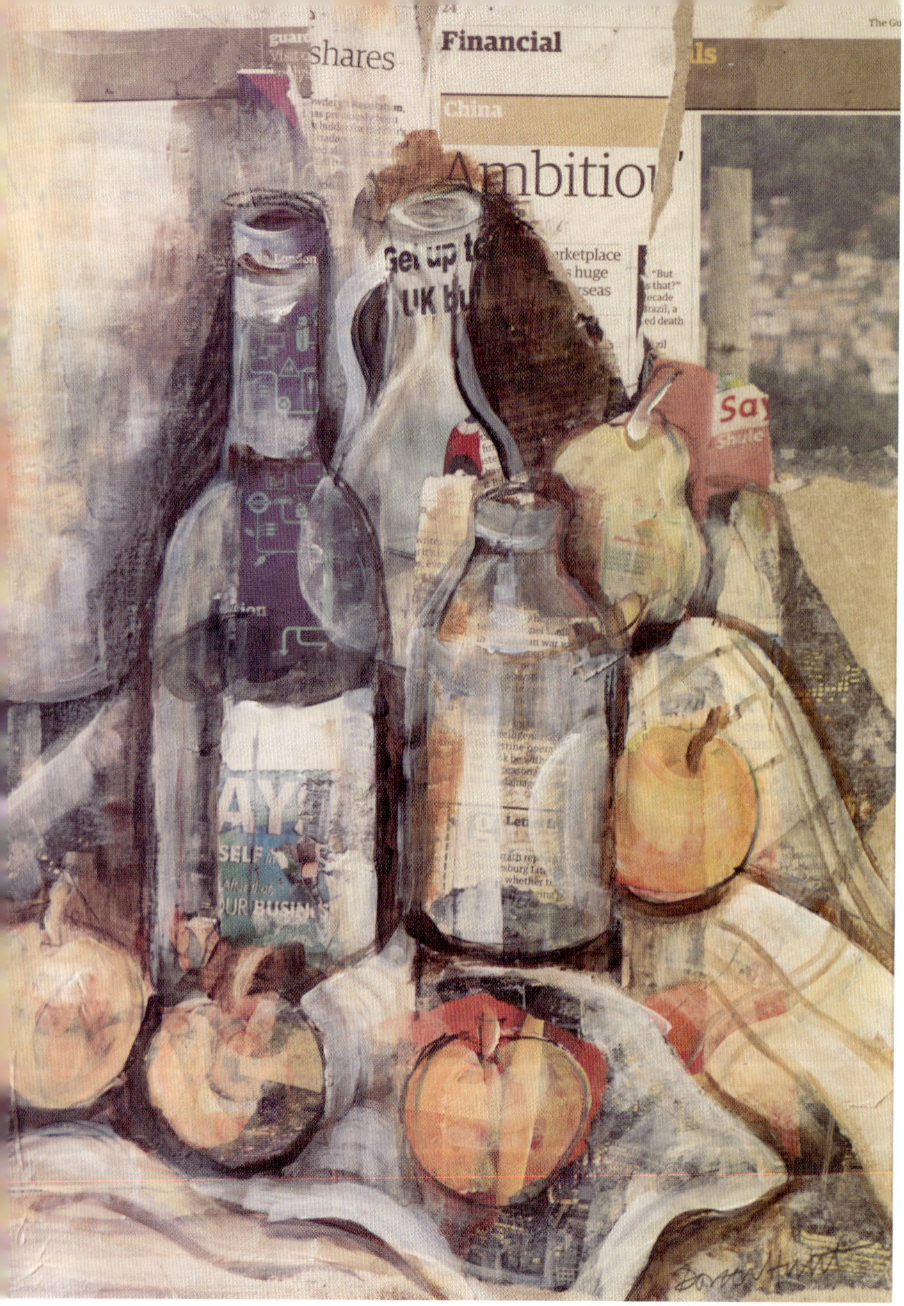

*Best Professional in the Still Life Category*

## Bottles And Fruit
*Doreen Hunt*

Mixed Media

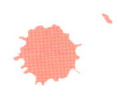

My work is developed from an actual still life group. Initially I did drawings to explore the composition then the resulting painting was done freely on the collage ground, again directly from the source. The colours have a basis in reality, but are not bound by it. The underlying collage contributes to the shapes and forms in the finished piece.

# September

**15**
Monday

**16**
Tuesday

**17**
Wednesday

**18**
Thursday

**19**
Friday

**20**
Saturday

**21**
Sunday

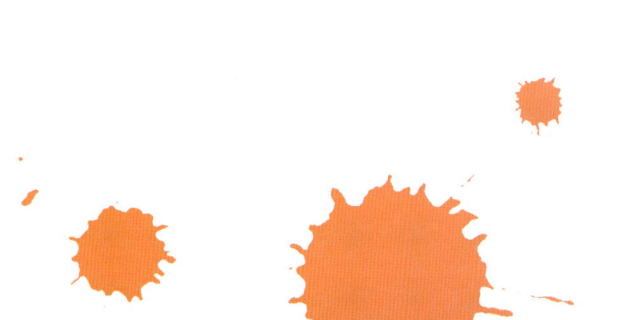

**SEPTEMBER**

| M | T | W | T | F | S | S |
|---|---|---|---|---|---|---|
| 1 | 2 | 3 | 4 | 5 | 6 | 7 |
| 8 | 9 | 10 | 11 | 12 | 13 | 14 |
| 15 | 16 | 17 | 18 | 19 | 20 | 21 |
| 22 | 23 | 24 | 25 | 26 | 27 | 28 |
| 29 | 30 | | | | | |

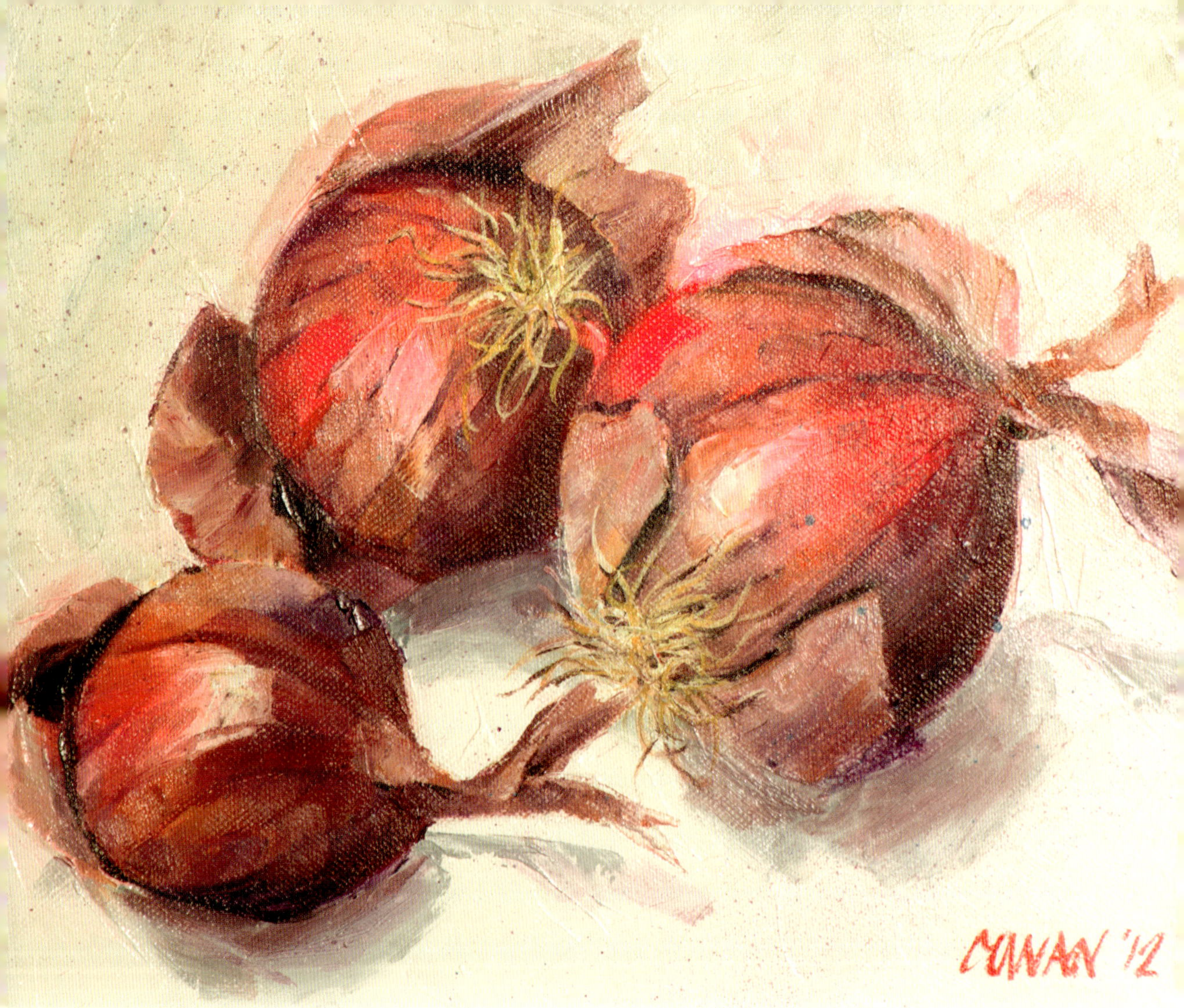

## Three Red Onions

*Brian Cowan*

Oils

Best Amateur in the Still Life Category

> *Three Red Onions* is a simple composition that forms a satisfying triangle of textured brush and knifework shapes on a neutral background. I found the ambient light source sufficient to give true colour, texture and form information. The piece was executed quickly with a spontaneity I really like to achieve.

www.cowanart.com

# September

**22**
Monday

**23**
Tuesday

**24**
Wednesday

**25**
Thursday

**26**
Friday

**27**
Saturday

**28**
Sunday

| SEPTEMBER | | | | | | |
|---|---|---|---|---|---|---|
| M | T | W | T | F | S | S |
| 1 | 2 | 3 | 4 | 5 | 6 | 7 |
| 8 | 9 | 10 | 11 | 12 | 13 | 14 |
| 15 | 16 | 17 | 18 | 19 | 20 | 21 |
| 22 | 23 | 24 | 25 | 26 | 27 | 28 |
| 29 | 30 | | | | | |

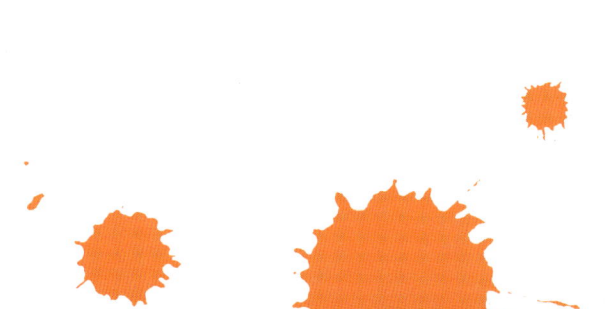

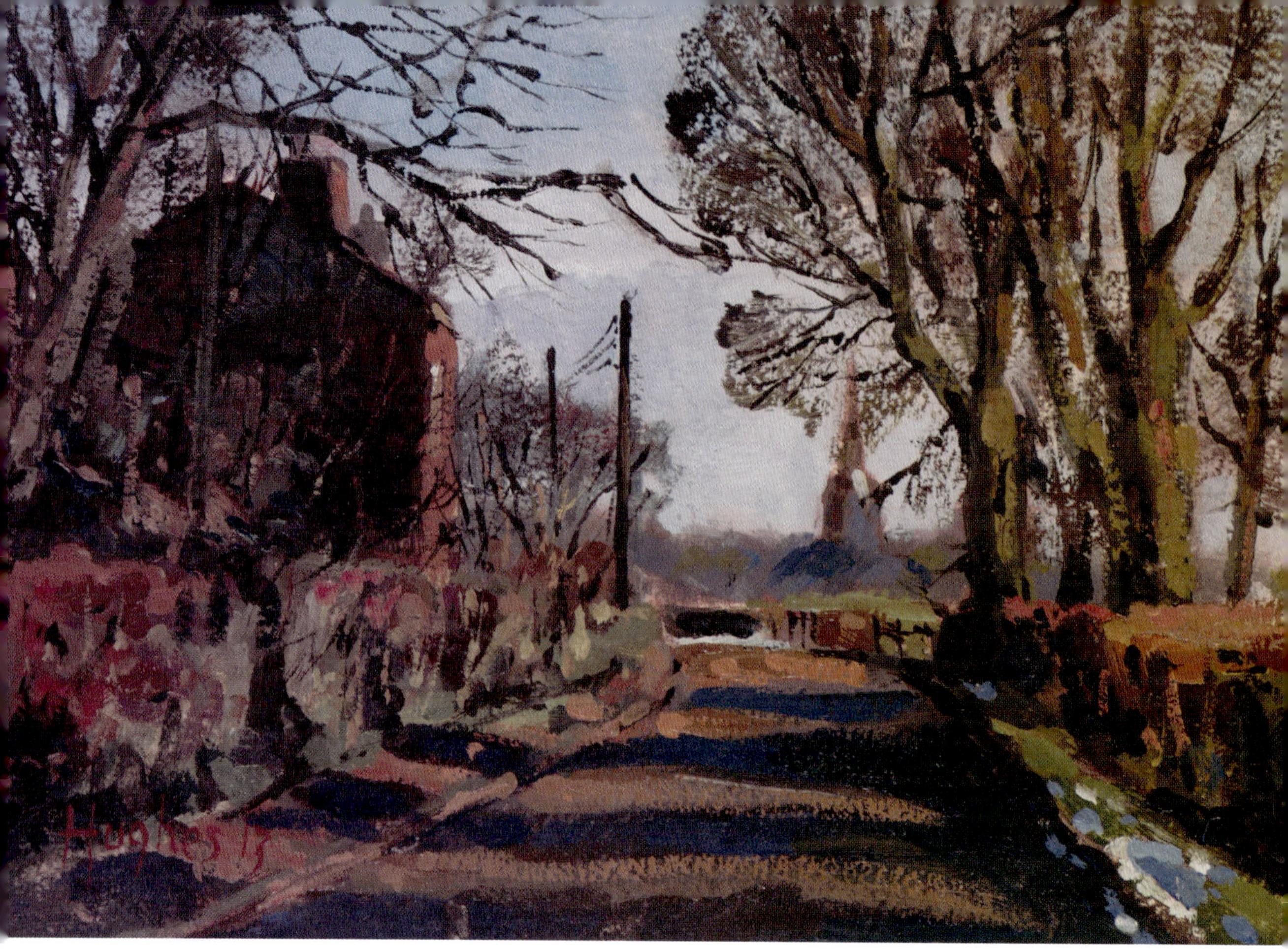

## Lunt Lane; 90 Minute Plein Air Painting
*Robert Hughes*

Acrylics

*Best Professional in the Landscape or Woodland Scene Category*

> I have driven through Lunt, which is a small community about half a mile from the church you see in the painting, on many occasions. On 22 January I met up with a fellow artist and we decided to paint the area around Lunt Lane. Having painted one scene in two hours, we then turned our attention to Lunt Lane itself, as the light was still fairly good. I painted Lunt Lane in 90 minutes.

www.bobhughesartist.com

# September/October

**29** Monday

**30** Tuesday

**1** Wednesday

**2** Thursday

**3** Friday

**4** Saturday

**5** Sunday

### OCTOBER

| M | T | W | T | F | S | S |
|---|---|---|---|---|---|---|
|   |   | 1 | 2 | 3 | 4 | 5 |
| 6 | 7 | 8 | 9 | 10 | 11 | 12 |
| 13 | 14 | 15 | 16 | 17 | 18 | 19 |
| 20 | 21 | 22 | 23 | 24 | 25 | 26 |
| 27 | 28 | 29 | 30 | 31 |   |   |

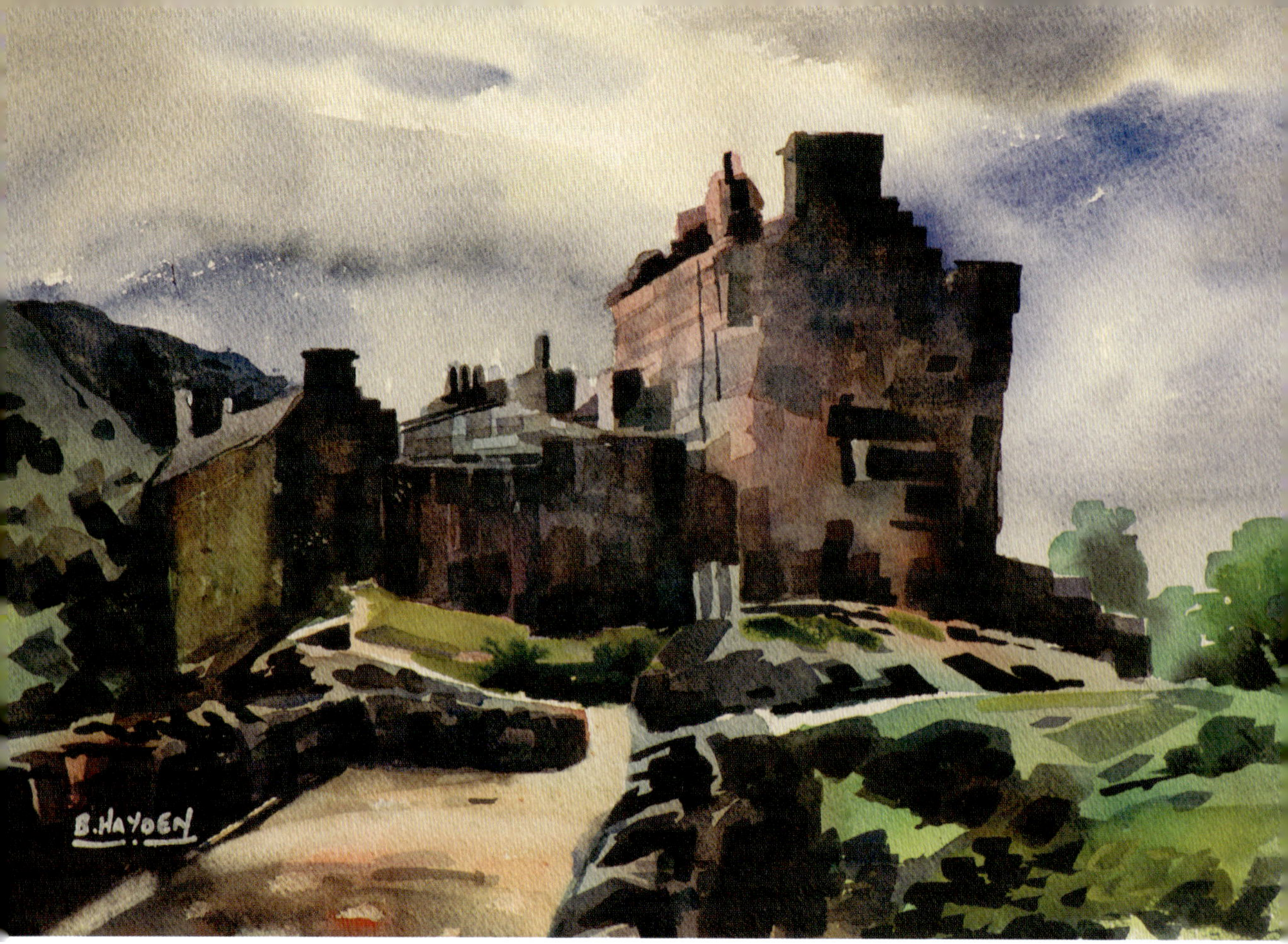

### Eilean Donan Castle
*Brigitte Hayden*
Watercolour

*Highly Commended*

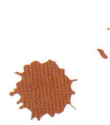

*Eilean Donan Castle* is an iconic Highland scene. I painted this with very little pre-drawing; instead I let the painting create itself using a limited palette and bold strokes. I think it is a strong and striking interpretation of Eilean Donan Castle – a watercolour with power and dynamism.

www.minigallery.co.uk/Brigitte_Hayden

# October

**6**
Monday

**7**
Tuesday

**8**
Wednesday

**9**
Thursday

**10**
Friday

**11**
Saturday

**12**
Sunday

### OCTOBER

| M | T | W | T | F | S | S |
|---|---|---|---|---|---|---|
|   |   | 1 | 2 | 3 | 4 | 5 |
| 6 | 7 | 8 | 9 | 10 | 11 | 12 |
| 13 | 14 | 15 | 16 | 17 | 18 | 19 |
| 20 | 21 | 22 | 23 | 24 | 25 | 26 |
| 27 | 28 | 29 | 30 | 31 |   |   |

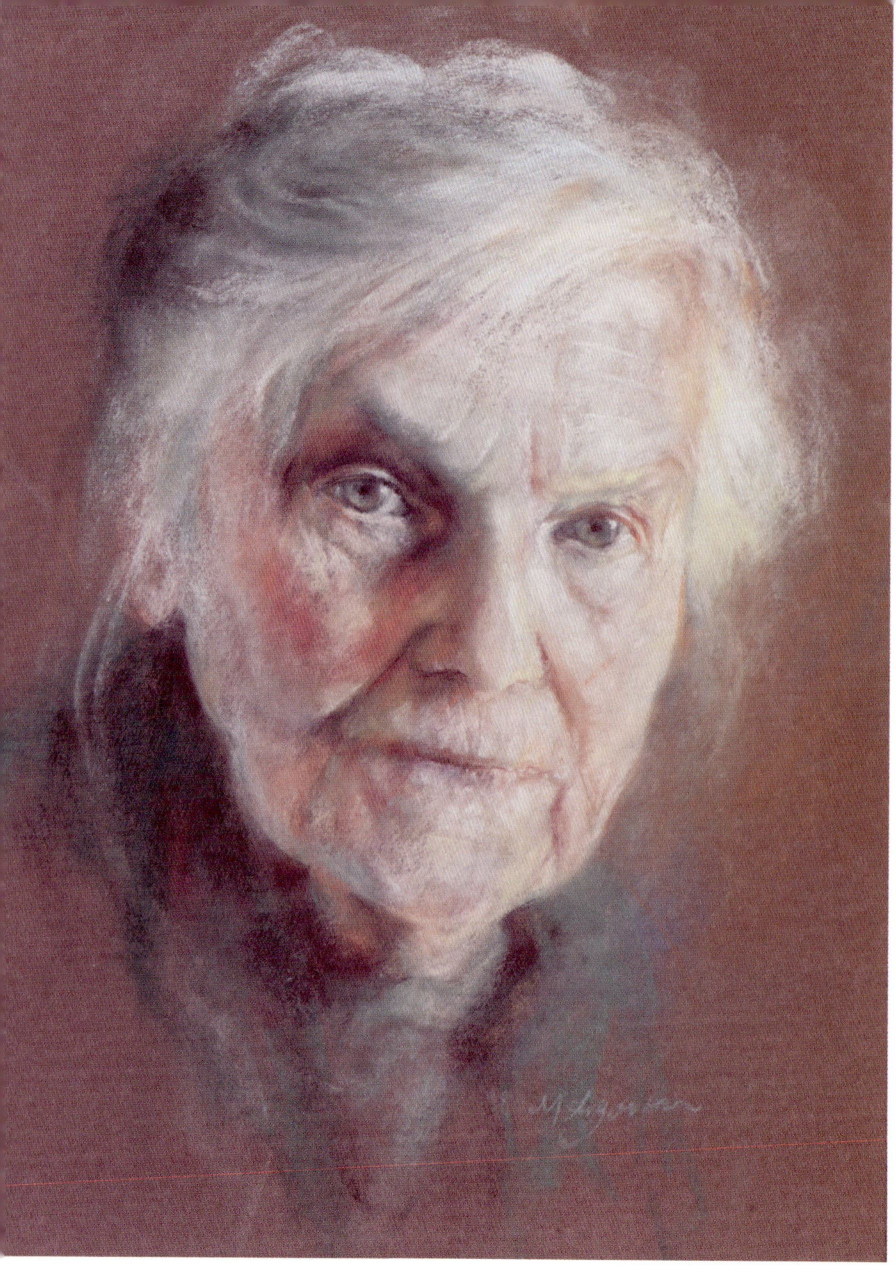

*Professional Artist of the Year*

## Firelight
*Margaret Ferguson*

Pastels

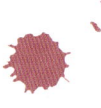

" I was fortunate to meet the model for this painting last year. She has a sparkling sense of fun and has a great skill in storytelling. I tried to capture these elements with pastel on sanded board while we shared an afternoon by the fire. "

www.margaretfergusonart.com

# October

*Columbus Day (US)*

**13**
Monday

**14**
Tuesday

**15**
Wednesday

**16**
Thursday

**17**
Friday

**18**
Saturday

**19**
Sunday

**OCTOBER**

| M | T | W | T | F | S | S |
|---|---|---|---|---|---|---|
|   |   | 1 | 2 | 3 | 4 | 5 |
| 6 | 7 | 8 | 9 | 10 | 11 | 12 |
| 13 | 14 | 15 | 16 | 17 | 18 | 19 |
| 20 | 21 | 22 | 23 | 24 | 25 | 26 |
| 27 | 28 | 29 | 30 | 31 |   |   |

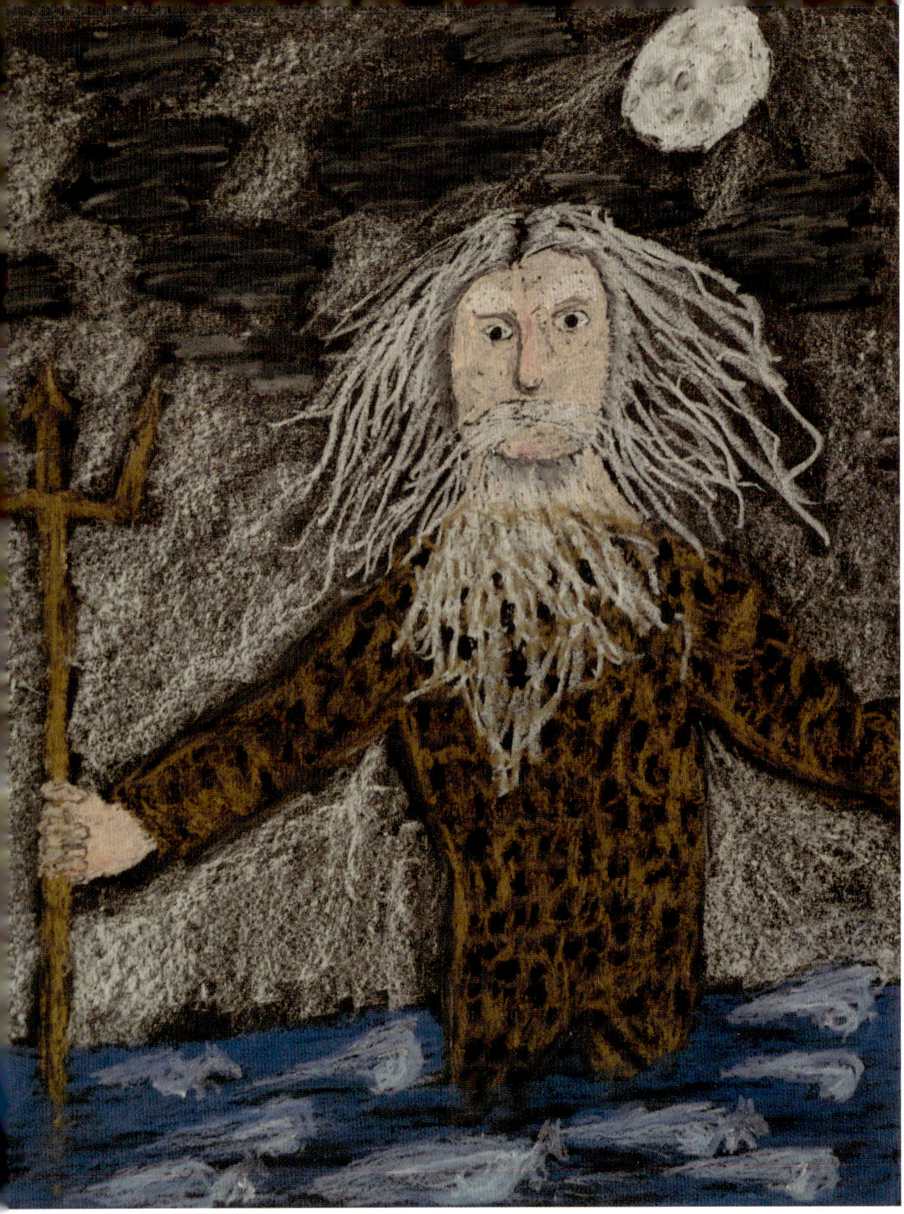

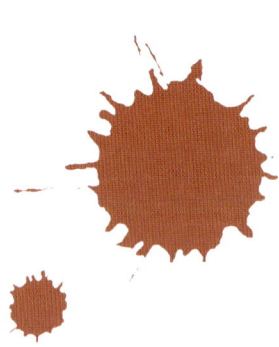

*Best Junior in the Portrait or Figure Category*

## Poseidon Rising From The Sea
*Hector Clarke*

*Oil Pastels*

 I was studying Greek mythology at school, and as part of my project I had to do a painting of a Greek god. Because I like the marine theme I chose Poseidon, the god of the sea. I tried to make him look powerful and dramatic rising out of the sea, covered in his golden fish-scale armour.

# October

## 20
Monday

## 21
Tuesday

## 22
Wednesday

## 23
Thursday

## 24
Friday

## 25
Saturday

## 26
Sunday

**OCTOBER**

| M | T | W | T | F | S | S |
|---|---|---|---|---|---|---|
|   |   | 1 | 2 | 3 | 4 | 5 |
| 6 | 7 | 8 | 9 | 10 | 11 | 12 |
| 13 | 14 | 15 | 16 | 17 | 18 | 19 |
| 20 | 21 | 22 | 23 | 24 | 25 | 26 |
| 27 | 28 | 29 | 30 | 31 |   |   |

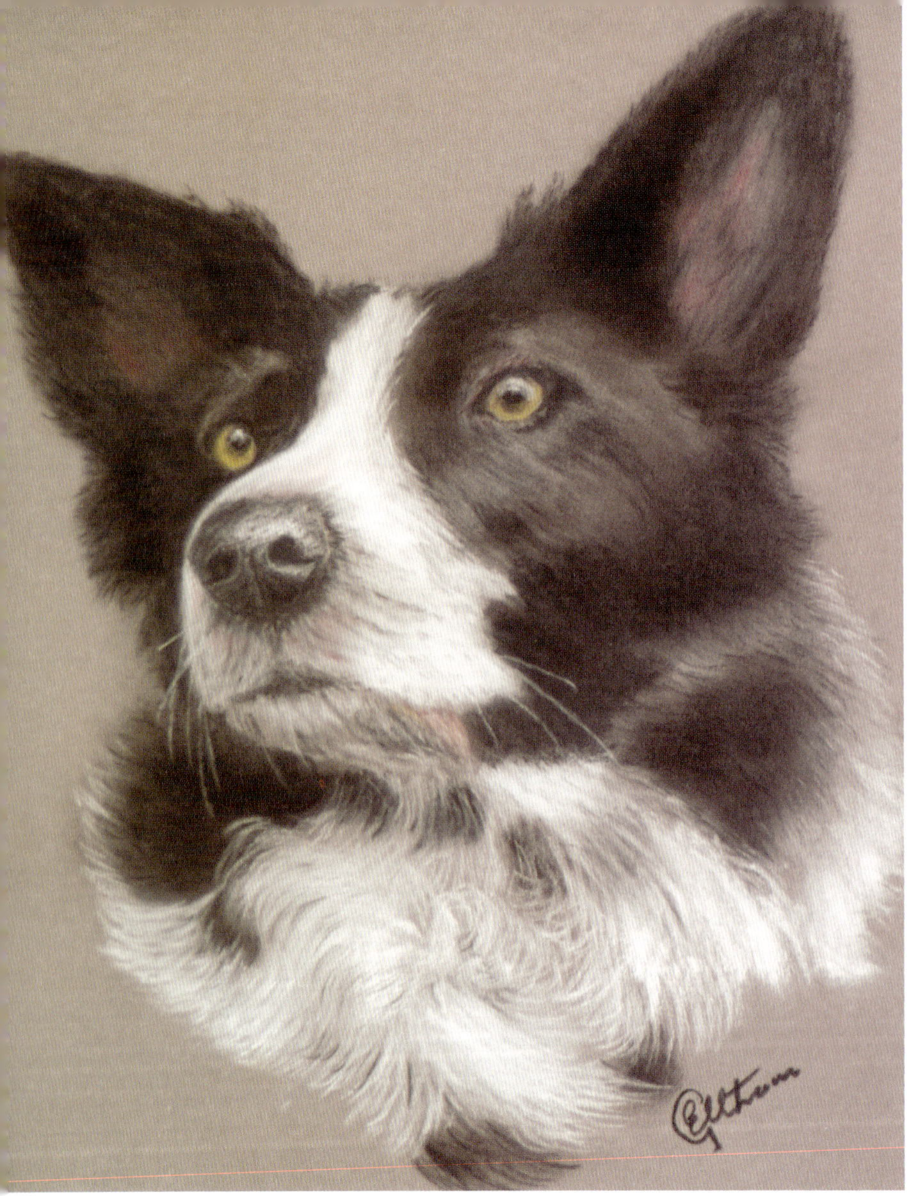

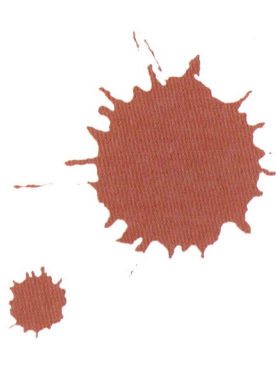

*June Atherton Beginner Award*

## Looking For You!!
*Geoff Eltham*

Pastels

" This was the first time I tried working in pastels and my first animal subject, made from a stock photo given to me by Vivien Walters to get me started. I booked a lesson with Vivien to see what using pastels was like; having only done a few landscapes in watercolour, I did find it challenging, but very enjoyable. I entered hoping for some constructive criticism. It's a little daunting how much I have to learn. "

# October/November

|  | 27 Monday |
|--|--|
|  | 28 Tuesday |
|  | 29 Wednesday |
|  | 30 Thursday |
| *Halloween* | 31 Friday |
|  | 1 Saturday |
|  | 2 Sunday |

**OCTOBER**

| M | T | W | T | F | S | S |
|---|---|---|---|---|---|---|
|   |   | 1 | 2 | 3 | 4 | 5 |
| 6 | 7 | 8 | 9 | 10 | 11 | 12 |
| 13 | 14 | 15 | 16 | 17 | 18 | 19 |
| 20 | 21 | 22 | 23 | 24 | 25 | 26 |
| 27 | 28 | 29 | 30 | 31 |   |   |

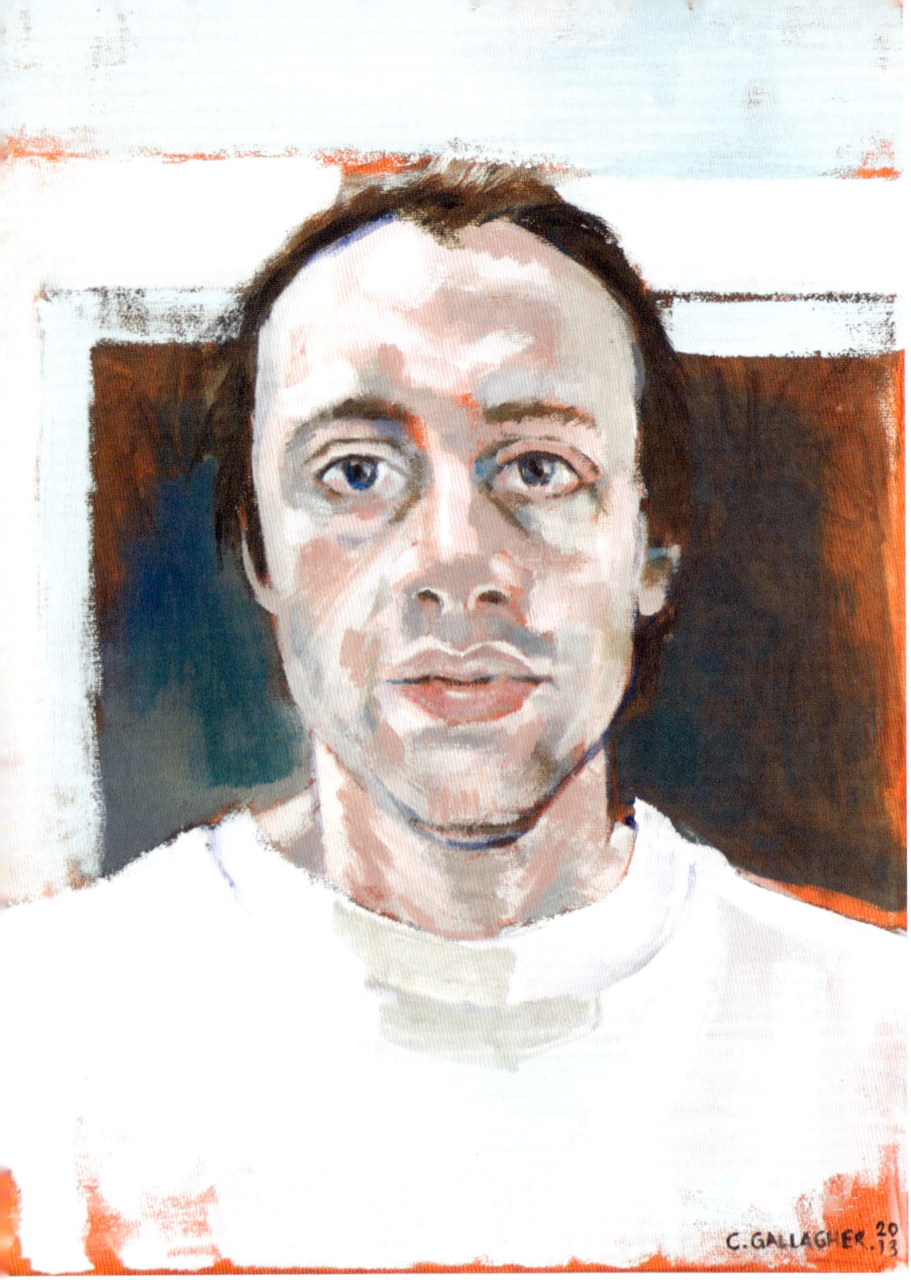

*Best Professional in the Portrait or Figure Category*

# Les
## *Christine Gallagher*
*Acrylics*

"I think of this work as an 'anti' portrait of my brother. Being camera shy, he allowed a single snapshot to work from, which I thought would be un-usable. However I found this pensive expression interesting, so decided to continue and make the painting. The alla prima style of brushwork reflects the immediacy of being allowed to take only one shot, which I feel lends a passport photo feel to the portrait."

www.cgallagherart.co.uk

# November

### 3
Monday

### 4
Tuesday

### 5
Wednesday

### 6
Thursday

### 7
Friday

### 8
Saturday

### 9
Sunday

| NOVEMBER | | | | | | |
|---|---|---|---|---|---|---|
| M | T | W | T | F | S | S |
|  |  |  |  |  | 1 | 2 |
| 3 | 4 | 5 | 6 | 7 | 8 | 9 |
| 10 | 11 | 12 | 13 | 14 | 15 | 16 |
| 17 | 18 | 19 | 20 | 21 | 22 | 23 |
| 24 | 25 | 26 | 27 | 28 | 29 | 30 |

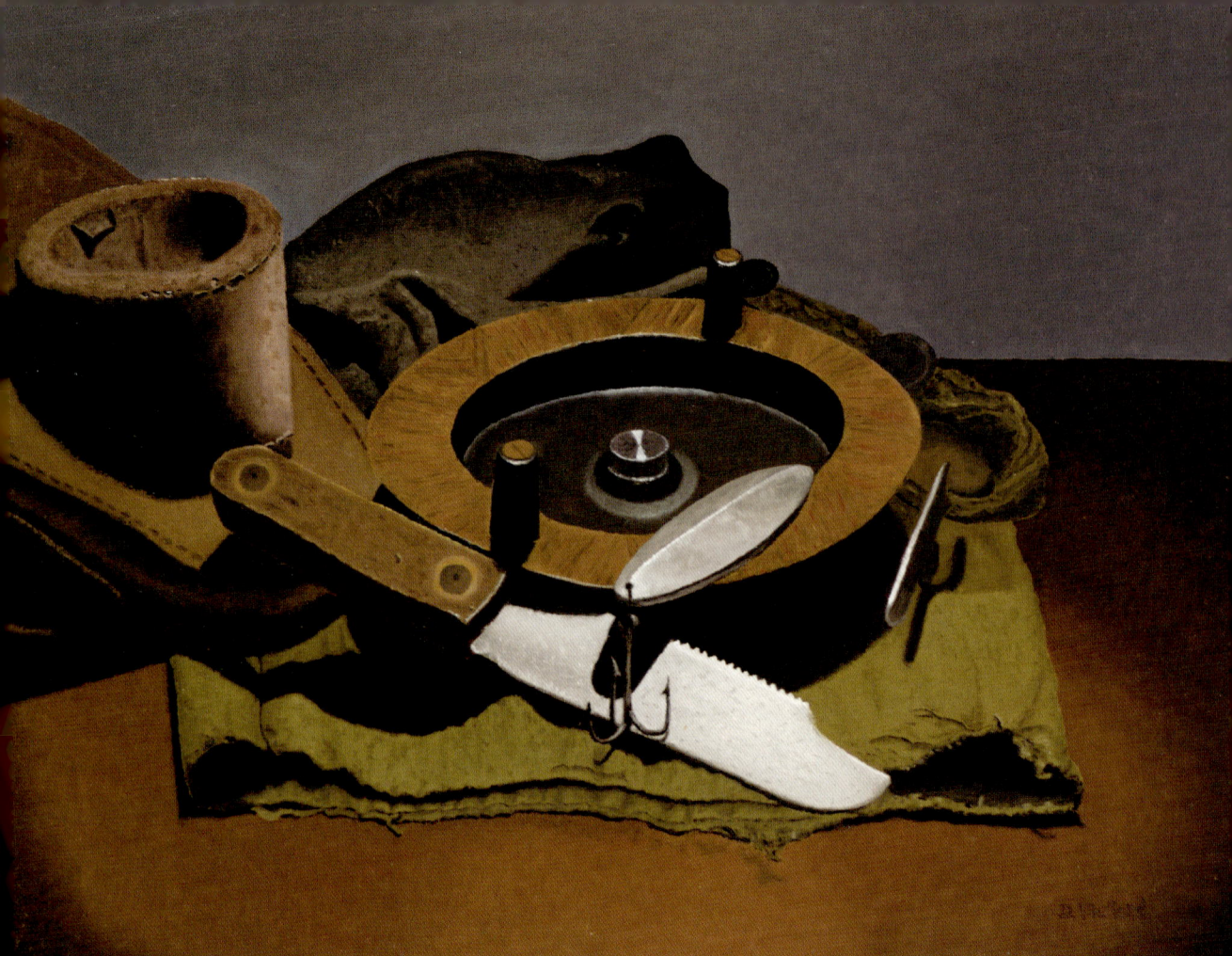

*Best Beginner in the Still Life Category*

# Gone Fishing
## D Mullard
Oils

> Many years ago, I fished in the Indian Ocean with the fishing gear in this picture. I was as passionate about rock and surf fishing then as I am about painting today, so it felt natural to combine the two passions. This being my third painting ever, I found drawing the reel and spinner technically demanding. I entered the painting as I identify with the subject matter in this more than that in my other still lifes.

# November

## 10
### Monday

*Veterans Day (US)*

## 11
### Tuesday

## 12
### Wednesday

## 13
### Thursday

## 14
### Friday

## 15
### Saturday

## 16
### Sunday

**NOVEMBER**

| M | T | W | T | F | S | S |
|---|---|---|---|---|---|---|
|   |   |   |   |   | 1 | 2 |
| 3 | 4 | 5 | 6 | 7 | 8 | 9 |
| 10 | 11 | 12 | 13 | 14 | 15 | 16 |
| 17 | 18 | 19 | 20 | 21 | 22 | 23 |
| 24 | 25 | 26 | 27 | 28 | 29 | 30 |

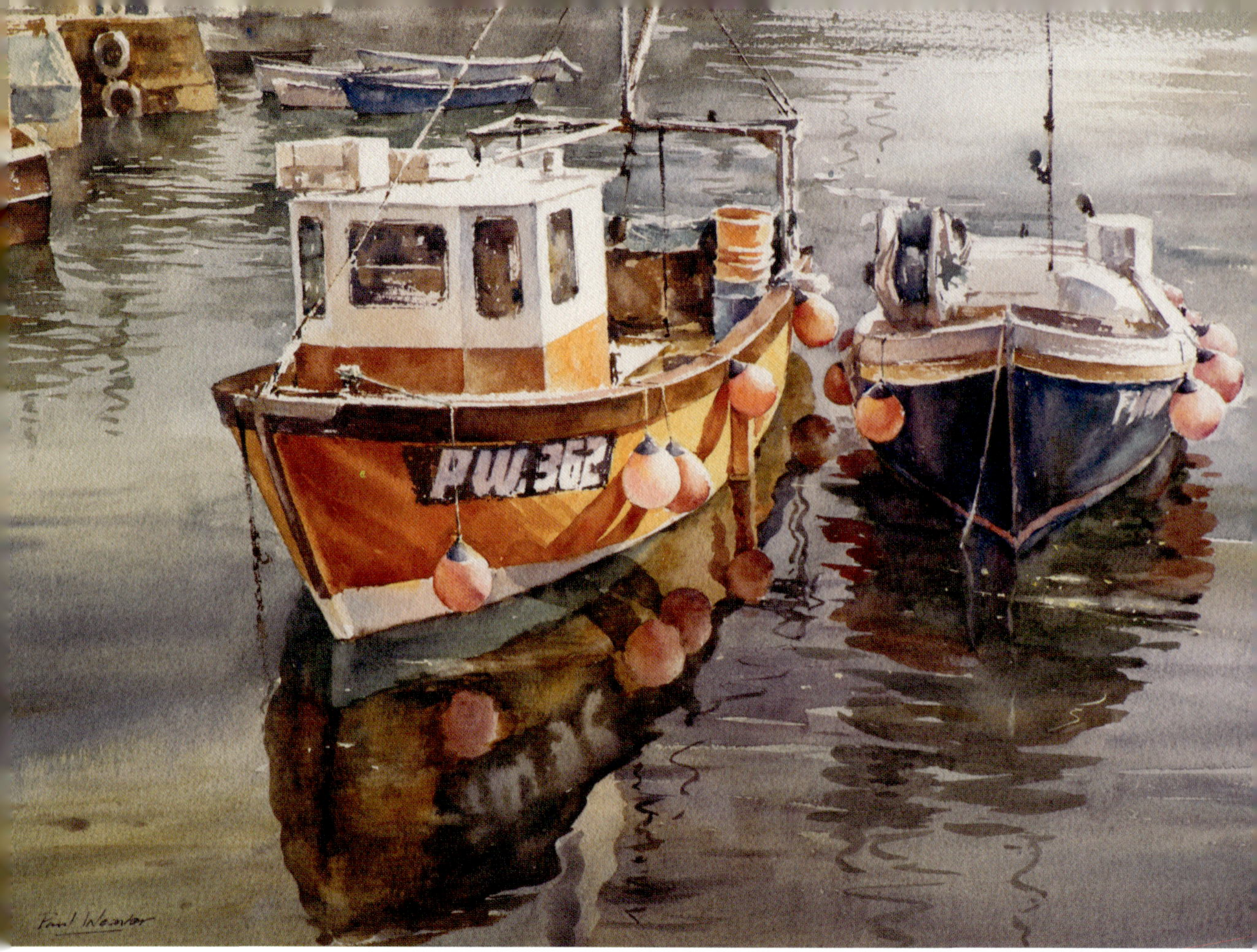

## Receding Tide, Mevagissey
*Paul Weaver*

*Watercolour*

*Waterscapes, Boats or Seascapes Category Winner*

" This was an early morning subject; I was inspired by the light striking the orange vessel, and the depth of tone seen in the reflections caused by the light and shallow water. I did a sketch on site and took several photographs, producing the final work back in the studio. I only realised that my initials were painted on the front of the orange boat halfway through! "

www.paulweaverart.co.uk

# November

**17**
Monday

**18**
Tuesday

**19**
Wednesday

**20**
Thursday

**21**
Friday

**22**
Saturday

**23**
Sunday

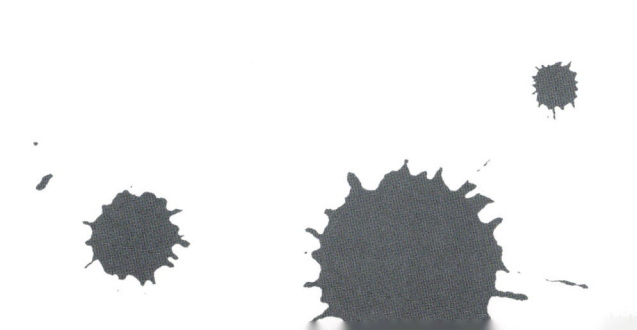

| NOVEMBER | | | | | | |
|---|---|---|---|---|---|---|
| M | T | W | T | F | S | S |
|  |  |  |  |  | 1 | 2 |
| 3 | 4 | 5 | 6 | 7 | 8 | 9 |
| 10 | 11 | 12 | 13 | 14 | 15 | 16 |
| 17 | 18 | 19 | 20 | 21 | 22 | 23 |
| 24 | 25 | 26 | 27 | 28 | 29 | 30 |

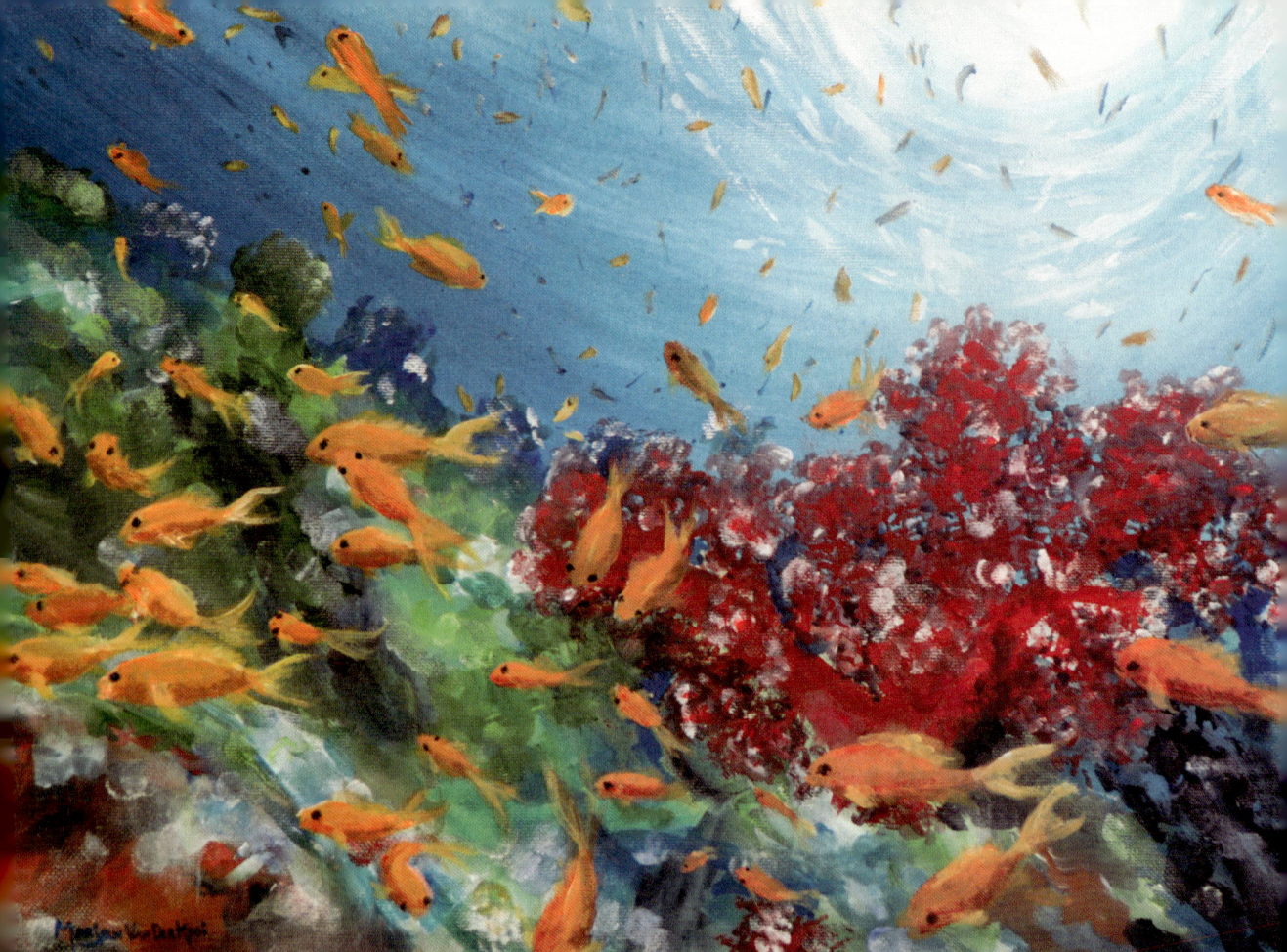

Highly Commended

## In The Sea

*Marjan Van Der Kooi*

Acrylics

> During a drab and grey time this winter I set out to make a cheerful painting to escape the cold spell. I subsequently painted *In The Sea* as I could imagine I was on vacation in some warm place, snorkelling in warm salty water. It was a fun painting to do, and I entered it so other people may enjoy it, too.

www.marjanvanderkooi.artweb.com

# November

**24**
Monday

**25**
Tuesday

**26**
Wednesday

*Thanksgiving (US)*

**27**
Thursday

**28**
Friday

**29**
Saturday

**30**
Sunday

| **NOVEMBER** | | | | | | |
|---|---|---|---|---|---|---|
| M | T | W | T | F | S | S |
|   |   |   |   |   | 1 | 2 |
| 3 | 4 | 5 | 6 | 7 | 8 | 9 |
| 10 | 11 | 12 | 13 | 14 | 15 | 16 |
| 17 | 18 | 19 | 20 | 21 | 22 | 23 |
| 24 | 25 | 26 | 27 | 28 | 29 | 30 |

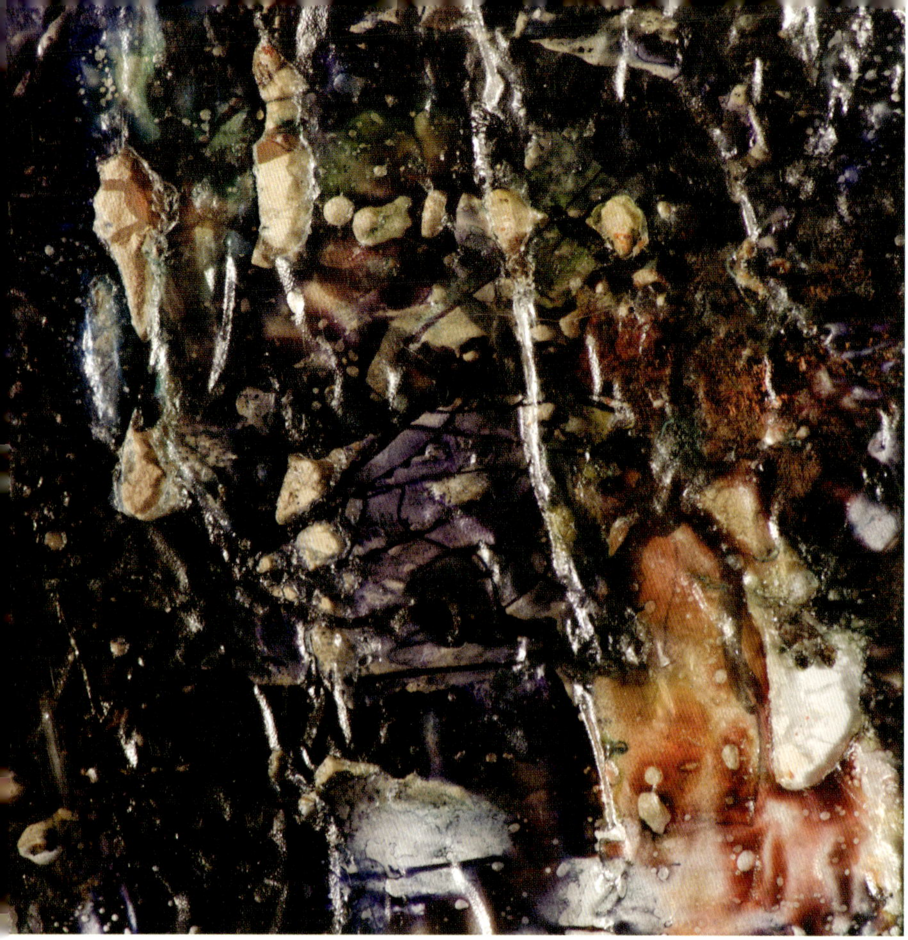

*Best Junior in the Abstract or Experimental Category*

## Close Up
*Jaydene Whelehan*

Mixed Media

> I have been exploring the theme of close-ups and have been particularly interested by the natural and harmonious patterns and colours evident in close ups of the brain. Neurons and their activity is fascinating. My piece was inspired by the artist Greg Dunn. I experimented with the materials and techniques. I used plastic, PVA glue, and Brushio inks which is why I have submitted it into the Abstract and Experimental category.

# December

**1**
Monday

**2**
Tuesday

**3**
Wednesday

**4**
Thursday

**5**
Friday

**6**
Saturday

**7**
Sunday

### DECEMBER

| M | T | W | T | F | S | S |
|---|---|---|---|---|---|---|
| 1 | 2 | 3 | 4 | 5 | 6 | 7 |
| 8 | 9 | 10 | 11 | 12 | 13 | 14 |
| 15 | 16 | 17 | 18 | 19 | 20 | 21 |
| 22 | 23 | 24 | 25 | 26 | 27 | 28 |
| 29 | 30 | 31 | | | | |

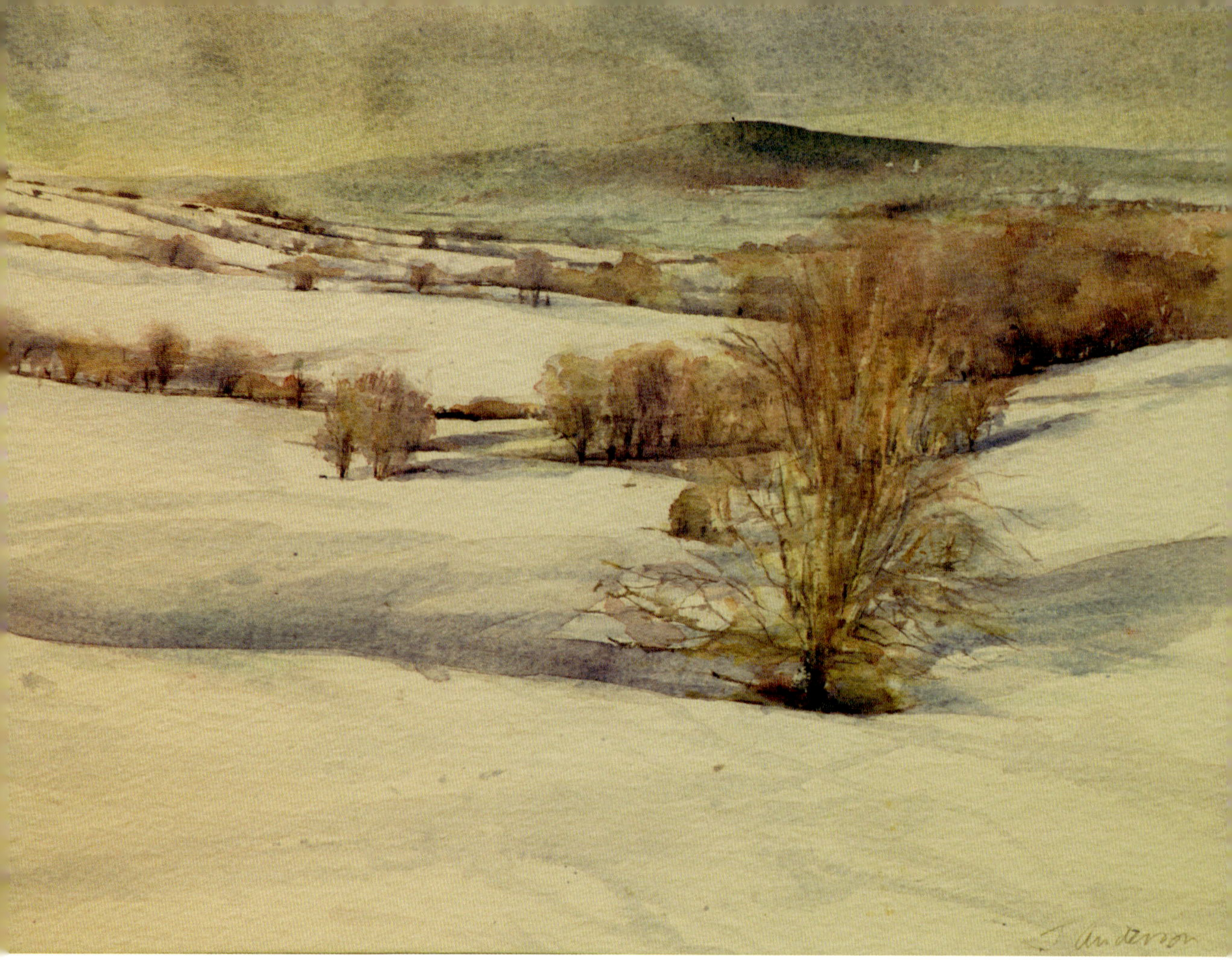

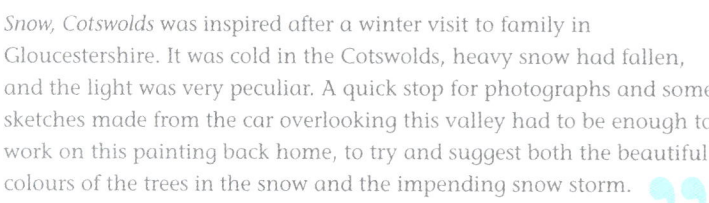

*Landscape or Woodland Scene Category Winner*

## Snow, Cotswolds

### J E Anderson Wood

*Watercolour*

> *Snow, Cotswolds* was inspired after a winter visit to family in Gloucestershire. It was cold in the Cotswolds, heavy snow had fallen, and the light was very peculiar. A quick stop for photographs and some sketches made from the car overlooking this valley had to be enough to work on this painting back home, to try and suggest both the beautiful colours of the trees in the snow and the impending snow storm.

www.janeandersonwood.co.uk

# December

**8**
Monday

**9**
Tuesday

**10**
Wednesday

**11**
Thursday

**12**
Friday

**13**
Saturday

**14**
Sunday

### DECEMBER

| M | T | W | T | F | S | S |
|---|---|---|---|---|---|---|
| 1 | 2 | 3 | 4 | 5 | 6 | 7 |
| 8 | 9 | 10 | 11 | 12 | 13 | 14 |
| 15 | 16 | 17 | 18 | 19 | 20 | 21 |
| 22 | 23 | 24 | 25 | 26 | 27 | 28 |
| 29 | 30 | 31 | | | | |

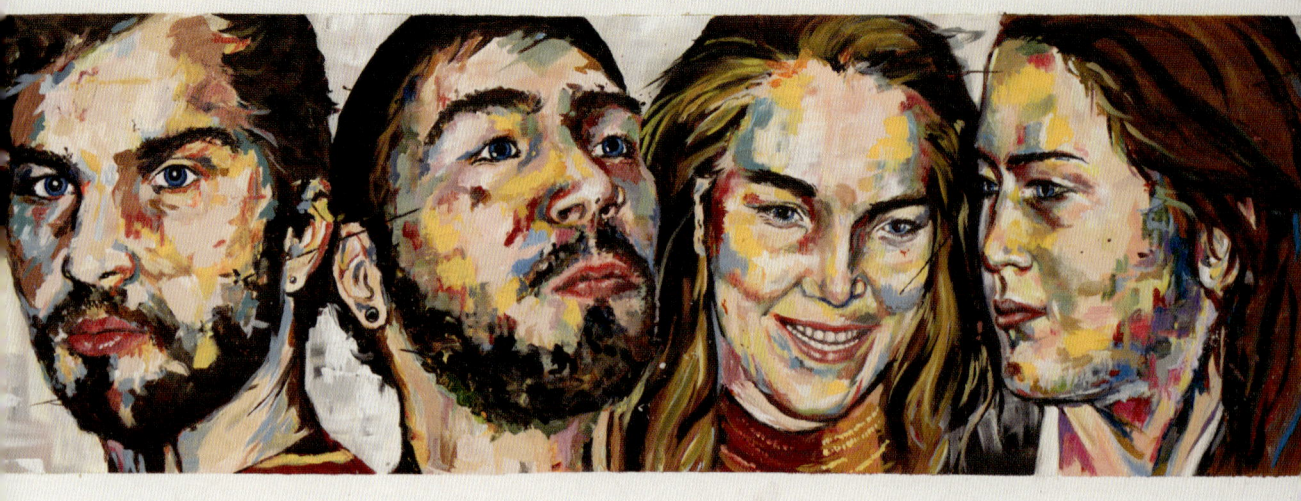

## My Siblings and I
*Katie Copley*

Acrylics

*Best Young in the Portrait or Figure Category*

> This painting was created for my final piece using the topic 'interrogating the object', in which I decided to do the human figure. The artist I used for inspiration was Andrew Salgado, who uses heavy brushstrokes and bright colours; he also uses a palette knife to create smudging between faces and the background. I decided to enter the piece as I thought it related to my theme of the human figure very well, and I thought it looked very effective with the faces all looking in different directions.

# December

**15**
Monday

**16**
Tuesday

**17**
Wednesday

**18**
Thursday

**19**
Friday

**20**
Saturday

**21**
Sunday

| **DECEMBER** | | | | | | |
| M | T | W | T | F | S | S |
| 1 | 2 | 3 | 4 | 5 | 6 | 7 |
| 8 | 9 | 10 | 11 | 12 | 13 | 14 |
| 15 | 16 | 17 | 18 | 19 | 20 | 21 |
| 22 | 23 | 24 | 25 | 26 | 27 | 28 |
| 29 | 30 | 31 | | | | |

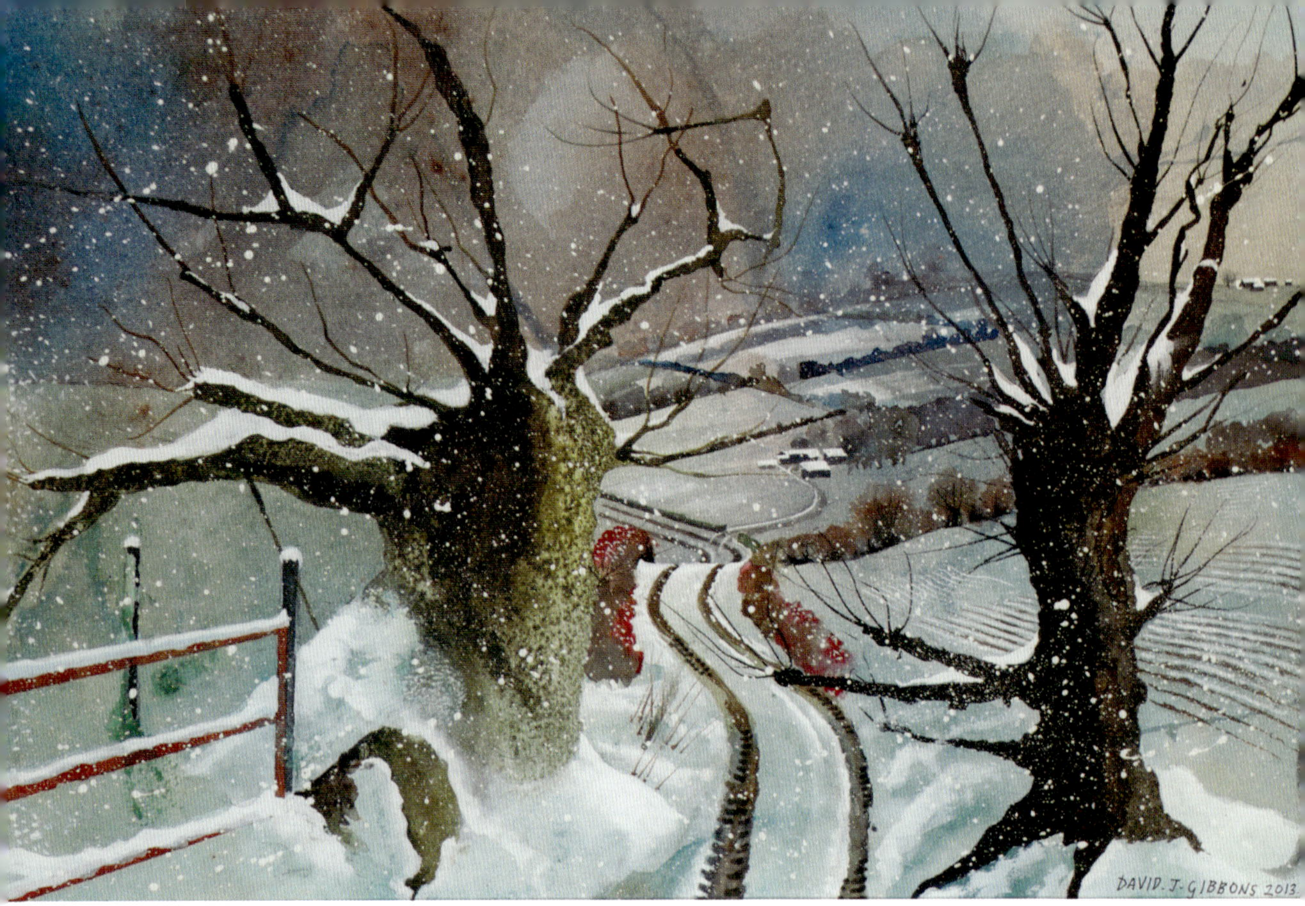

*Highly Commended*

## Weird Winter
*David Gibbons*
Watercolour

 This started as an abstract with a large splash of brown, sprinkled with salt and blown with a hairdryer, together with light blue washes. This suggested a winter scene, so I added a second tree to create an entrance pathway leading into a valley, towards the farmhouse and hills. I then laid much stronger washes to provide a contrast for the snow and enhance the weird winter light. Finally, I toothbrushed snowflakes over the whole piece.

www.davidgibbons.weebly.com

# December

22
Monday

23
Tuesday

24
Wednesday

*Christmas Day*

25
Thursday

*Boxing Day (UK, Aus)*

26
Friday

27
Saturday

28
Sunday

**DECEMBER**

| M | T | W | T | F | S | S |
|---|---|---|---|---|---|---|
| 1 | 2 | 3 | 4 | 5 | 6 | 7 |
| 8 | 9 | 10 | 11 | 12 | 13 | 14 |
| 15 | 16 | 17 | 18 | 19 | 20 | 21 |
| 22 | 23 | 24 | 25 | 26 | 27 | 28 |
| 29 | 30 | 31 | | | | |

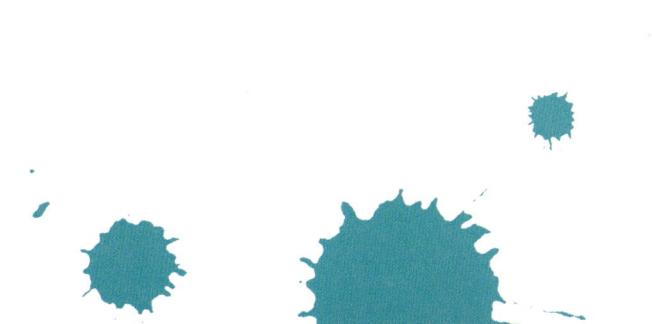

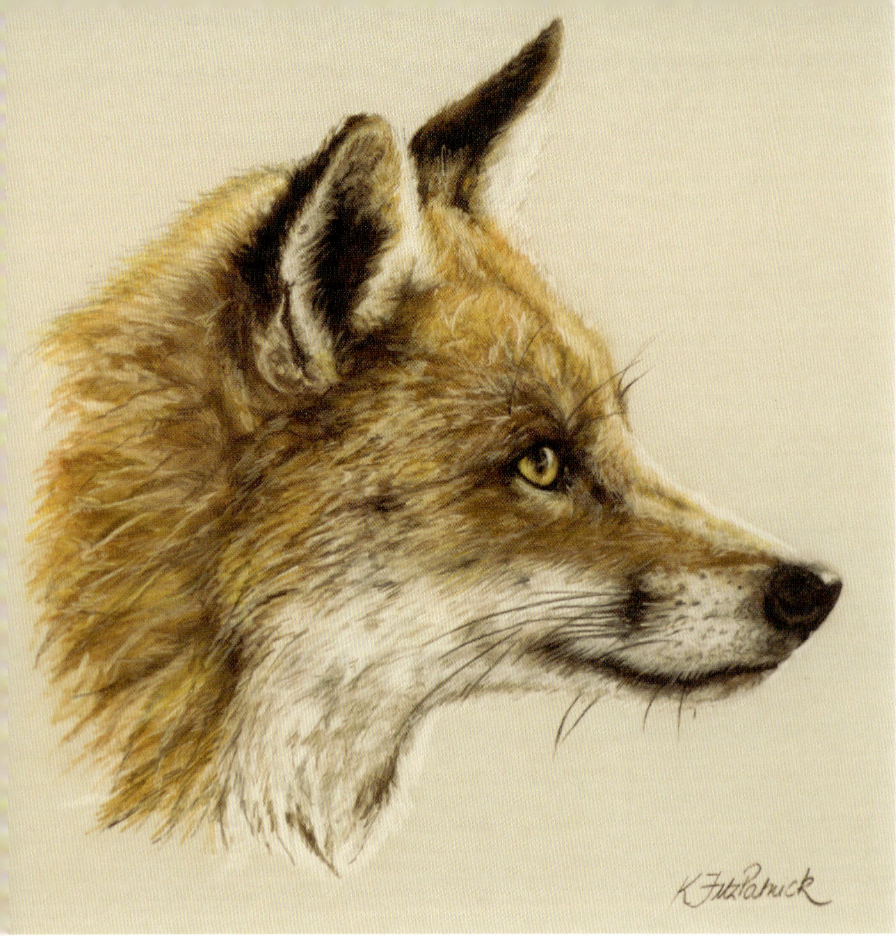

*Best Beginner in the Animal or Wildlife Category*

# Red Fox II

*Kirstie Fitzpatrick*

*Pastels*

> My painting *Red Fox II* was inspired by a beautiful photograph by British wildlife photographer David J Slater. I particularly love working on paintings that capture our native wildlife: the surprised expression of a wild brown hare, caught in a summer meadow; the knowing wisdom of the owl; and, of course, the wily mischievousness of the red fox. Whilst I have painted more exotic animals, it is always our native British species that speak to me most.

# December / January

**29** Monday

**30** Tuesday

**31** Wednesday

*New Year's Day*

**1** Thursday

**2** Friday

**3** Saturday

**4** Sunday

### JANUARY 2015

| M | T | W | T | F | S | S |
|---|---|---|---|---|---|---|
|   |   |   | 1 | 2 | 3 | 4 |
| 5 | 6 | 7 | 8 | 9 | 10 | 11 |
| 12 | 13 | 14 | 15 | 16 | 17 | 18 |
| 19 | 20 | 21 | 22 | 23 | 24 | 25 |
| 26 | 27 | 28 | 29 | 30 | 31 |   |

# 2014 Planner

|   | JANUARY | FEBRUARY | MARCH | APRIL | MAY | JUNE |
|---|---------|----------|-------|-------|-----|------|
| M |    |    |    |    |    |    |
| T |    |    |    | 1  |    |    |
| W | 1  |    |    | 2  |    |    |
| T | 2  |    |    | 3  | 1  |    |
| F | 3  |    |    | 4  | 2  |    |
| S | 4  | 1  | 1  | 5  | 3  |    |
| S | 5  | 2  | 2  | 6  | 4  | 1  |
| M | 6  | 3  | 3  | 7  | 5  | 2  |
| T | 7  | 4  | 4  | 8  | 6  | 3  |
| W | 8  | 5  | 5  | 9  | 7  | 4  |
| T | 9  | 6  | 6  | 10 | 8  | 5  |
| F | 10 | 7  | 7  | 11 | 9  | 6  |
| S | 11 | 8  | 8  | 12 | 10 | 7  |
| S | 12 | 9  | 9  | 13 | 11 | 8  |
| M | 13 | 10 | 10 | 14 | 12 | 9  |
| T | 14 | 11 | 11 | 15 | 13 | 10 |
| W | 15 | 12 | 12 | 16 | 14 | 11 |
| T | 16 | 13 | 13 | 17 | 15 | 12 |
| F | 17 | 14 | 14 | 18 | 16 | 13 |
| S | 18 | 15 | 15 | 19 | 17 | 14 |
| S | 19 | 16 | 16 | 20 | 18 | 15 |
| M | 20 | 17 | 17 | 21 | 19 | 16 |
| T | 21 | 18 | 18 | 22 | 20 | 17 |
| W | 22 | 19 | 19 | 23 | 21 | 18 |
| T | 23 | 20 | 20 | 24 | 22 | 19 |
| F | 24 | 21 | 21 | 25 | 23 | 20 |
| S | 25 | 22 | 22 | 26 | 24 | 21 |
| S | 26 | 23 | 23 | 27 | 25 | 22 |
| M | 27 | 24 | 24 | 28 | 26 | 23 |
| T | 28 | 25 | 25 | 29 | 27 | 24 |
| W | 29 | 26 | 26 | 30 | 28 | 25 |
| T | 30 | 27 | 27 |    | 29 | 26 |
| F | 31 | 28 | 28 |    | 30 | 27 |
| S |    |    | 29 |    | 31 | 28 |
| S |    |    | 30 |    |    | 29 |
| M |    |    | 31 |    |    | 30 |
| T |    |    |    |    |    |    |

|   | JULY | AUGUST | SEPTEMBER | OCTOBER | NOVEMBER | DECEMBER |
|---|---|---|---|---|---|---|
| M |  |  | 1 |  |  | 1 |
| T | 1 |  | 2 |  |  | 2 |
| W | 2 |  | 3 | 1 |  | 3 |
| T | 3 |  | 4 | 2 |  | 4 |
| F | 4 | 1 | 5 | 3 |  | 5 |
| S | 5 | 2 | 6 | 4 | 1 | 6 |
| S | 6 | 3 | 7 | 5 | 2 | 7 |
| M | 7 | 4 | 8 | 6 | 3 | 8 |
| T | 8 | 5 | 9 | 7 | 4 | 9 |
| W | 9 | 6 | 10 | 8 | 5 | 10 |
| T | 10 | 7 | 11 | 9 | 6 | 11 |
| F | 11 | 8 | 12 | 10 | 7 | 12 |
| S | 12 | 9 | 13 | 11 | 8 | 13 |
| S | 13 | 10 | 14 | 12 | 9 | 14 |
| M | 14 | 11 | 15 | 13 | 10 | 15 |
| T | 15 | 12 | 16 | 14 | 11 | 16 |
| W | 16 | 13 | 17 | 15 | 12 | 17 |
| T | 17 | 14 | 18 | 16 | 13 | 18 |
| F | 18 | 15 | 19 | 17 | 14 | 19 |
| S | 19 | 16 | 20 | 18 | 15 | 20 |
| S | 20 | 17 | 21 | 19 | 16 | 21 |
| M | 21 | 18 | 22 | 20 | 17 | 22 |
| T | 22 | 19 | 23 | 21 | 18 | 23 |
| W | 23 | 20 | 24 | 22 | 19 | 24 |
| T | 24 | 21 | 25 | 23 | 20 | 25 |
| F | 25 | 22 | 26 | 24 | 21 | 26 |
| S | 26 | 23 | 27 | 25 | 22 | 27 |
| S | 27 | 24 | 28 | 26 | 23 | 28 |
| M | 28 | 25 | 29 | 27 | 24 | 29 |
| T | 29 | 26 | 30 | 28 | 25 | 30 |
| W | 30 | 27 |  | 29 | 26 | 31 |
| T | 31 | 28 |  | 30 | 27 |  |
| F |  | 29 |  | 31 | 28 |  |
| S |  | 30 |  |  | 29 |  |
| S |  | 31 |  |  | 30 |  |
| M |  |  |  |  |  |  |
| T |  |  |  |  |  |  |

# 2015 Planner

|   | JANUARY | FEBRUARY | MARCH | APRIL | MAY | JUNE |
|---|---|---|---|---|---|---|
| M |   |   |   |   |   | 1 |
| T |   |   |   |   |   | 2 |
| W |   |   |   | 1 |   | 3 |
| T | 1 |   |   | 2 |   | 4 |
| F | 2 |   |   | 3 | 1 | 5 |
| S | 3 |   |   | 4 | 2 | 6 |
| S | 4 | 1 | 1 | 5 | 3 | 7 |
| M | 5 | 2 | 2 | 6 | 4 | 8 |
| T | 6 | 3 | 3 | 7 | 5 | 9 |
| W | 7 | 4 | 4 | 8 | 6 | 10 |
| T | 8 | 5 | 5 | 9 | 7 | 11 |
| F | 9 | 6 | 6 | 10 | 8 | 12 |
| S | 10 | 7 | 7 | 11 | 9 | 13 |
| S | 11 | 8 | 8 | 12 | 10 | 14 |
| M | 12 | 9 | 9 | 13 | 11 | 15 |
| T | 13 | 10 | 10 | 14 | 12 | 16 |
| W | 14 | 11 | 11 | 15 | 13 | 17 |
| T | 15 | 12 | 12 | 16 | 14 | 18 |
| F | 16 | 13 | 13 | 17 | 15 | 19 |
| S | 17 | 14 | 14 | 18 | 16 | 20 |
| S | 18 | 15 | 15 | 19 | 17 | 21 |
| M | 19 | 16 | 16 | 20 | 18 | 22 |
| T | 20 | 17 | 17 | 21 | 19 | 23 |
| W | 21 | 18 | 18 | 22 | 20 | 24 |
| T | 22 | 19 | 19 | 23 | 21 | 25 |
| F | 23 | 20 | 20 | 24 | 22 | 26 |
| S | 24 | 21 | 21 | 25 | 23 | 27 |
| S | 25 | 22 | 22 | 26 | 24 | 28 |
| M | 26 | 23 | 23 | 27 | 25 | 29 |
| T | 27 | 24 | 24 | 28 | 26 | 30 |
| W | 28 | 25 | 25 | 29 | 27 |   |
| T | 29 | 26 | 26 | 30 | 28 |   |
| F | 30 | 27 | 27 |   | 29 |   |
| S | 31 | 28 | 28 |   | 30 |   |
| S |   |   | 29 |   | 31 |   |
| M |   |   | 30 |   |   |   |
| T |   |   | 31 |   |   |   |

|   | JULY | AUGUST | SEPTEMBER | OCTOBER | NOVEMBER | DECEMBER |
|---|---|---|---|---|---|---|
| M |    |    |    |    |    |    |
| T |    |    | 1  |    |    | 1  |
| W | 1  |    | 2  |    |    | 2  |
| T | 2  |    | 3  | 1  |    | 3  |
| F | 3  |    | 4  | 2  |    | 4  |
| S | 4  | 1  | 5  | 3  |    | 5  |
| S | 5  | 2  | 6  | 4  | 1  | 6  |
| M | 6  | 3  | 7  | 5  | 2  | 7  |
| T | 7  | 4  | 8  | 6  | 3  | 8  |
| W | 8  | 5  | 9  | 7  | 4  | 9  |
| T | 9  | 6  | 10 | 8  | 5  | 10 |
| F | 10 | 7  | 11 | 9  | 6  | 11 |
| S | 11 | 8  | 12 | 10 | 7  | 12 |
| S | 12 | 9  | 13 | 11 | 8  | 13 |
| M | 13 | 10 | 14 | 12 | 9  | 14 |
| T | 14 | 11 | 15 | 13 | 10 | 15 |
| W | 15 | 12 | 16 | 14 | 11 | 16 |
| T | 16 | 13 | 17 | 15 | 12 | 17 |
| F | 17 | 14 | 18 | 16 | 13 | 18 |
| S | 18 | 15 | 19 | 17 | 14 | 19 |
| S | 19 | 16 | 20 | 18 | 15 | 20 |
| M | 20 | 17 | 21 | 19 | 16 | 21 |
| T | 21 | 18 | 22 | 20 | 17 | 22 |
| W | 22 | 19 | 23 | 21 | 18 | 23 |
| T | 23 | 20 | 24 | 22 | 19 | 24 |
| F | 24 | 21 | 25 | 23 | 20 | 25 |
| S | 25 | 22 | 26 | 24 | 21 | 26 |
| S | 26 | 23 | 27 | 25 | 22 | 27 |
| M | 27 | 24 | 28 | 26 | 23 | 28 |
| T | 28 | 25 | 29 | 27 | 24 | 29 |
| W | 29 | 26 | 30 | 28 | 25 | 30 |
| T | 30 | 27 |    | 29 | 26 | 31 |
| F | 31 | 28 |    | 30 | 27 |    |
| S |    | 29 |    | 31 | 28 |    |
| S |    | 30 |    |    | 29 |    |
| M |    | 31 |    |    | 30 |    |
| T |    |    |    |    |    |    |

# 2015

## JANUARY
| M | T | W | T | F | S | S |
|---|---|---|---|---|---|---|
|   |   |   | 1 | 2 | 3 | 4 |
| 5 | 6 | 7 | 8 | 9 | 10 | 11 |
| 12 | 13 | 14 | 15 | 16 | 17 | 18 |
| 19 | 20 | 21 | 22 | 23 | 24 | 25 |
| 26 | 27 | 28 | 29 | 30 | 31 |   |

## FEBRUARY
| M | T | W | T | F | S | S |
|---|---|---|---|---|---|---|
|   |   |   |   |   |   | 1 |
| 2 | 3 | 4 | 5 | 6 | 7 | 8 |
| 9 | 10 | 11 | 12 | 13 | 14 | 15 |
| 16 | 17 | 18 | 19 | 20 | 21 | 22 |
| 23 | 24 | 25 | 26 | 27 | 28 |   |

## MARCH
| M | T | W | T | F | S | S |
|---|---|---|---|---|---|---|
|   |   |   |   |   |   | 1 |
| 2 | 3 | 4 | 5 | 6 | 7 | 8 |
| 9 | 10 | 11 | 12 | 13 | 14 | 15 |
| 16 | 17 | 18 | 19 | 20 | 21 | 22 |
| 23 | 24 | 25 | 26 | 27 | 28 | 29 |
| 30 | 31 |   |   |   |   |   |

## APRIL
| M | T | W | T | F | S | S |
|---|---|---|---|---|---|---|
|   |   | 1 | 2 | 3 | 4 | 5 |
| 6 | 7 | 8 | 9 | 10 | 11 | 12 |
| 13 | 14 | 15 | 16 | 17 | 18 | 19 |
| 20 | 21 | 22 | 23 | 24 | 25 | 26 |
| 27 | 28 | 29 | 30 |   |   |   |

## MAY
| M | T | W | T | F | S | S |
|---|---|---|---|---|---|---|
|   |   |   |   | 1 | 2 | 3 |
| 4 | 5 | 6 | 7 | 8 | 9 | 10 |
| 11 | 12 | 13 | 14 | 15 | 16 | 17 |
| 18 | 19 | 20 | 21 | 22 | 23 | 24 |
| 25 | 26 | 27 | 28 | 29 | 30 | 31 |

## JUNE
| M | T | W | T | F | S | S |
|---|---|---|---|---|---|---|
| 1 | 2 | 3 | 4 | 5 | 6 | 7 |
| 8 | 9 | 10 | 11 | 12 | 13 | 14 |
| 15 | 16 | 17 | 18 | 19 | 20 | 21 |
| 22 | 23 | 24 | 25 | 26 | 27 | 28 |
| 29 | 30 |   |   |   |   |   |

## JULY
| M | T | W | T | F | S | S |
|---|---|---|---|---|---|---|
|   |   | 1 | 2 | 3 | 4 | 5 |
| 6 | 7 | 8 | 9 | 10 | 11 | 12 |
| 13 | 14 | 15 | 16 | 17 | 18 | 19 |
| 20 | 21 | 22 | 23 | 24 | 25 | 26 |
| 27 | 28 | 29 | 30 | 31 |   |   |

## AUGUST
| M | T | W | T | F | S | S |
|---|---|---|---|---|---|---|
|   |   |   |   |   | 1 | 2 |
| 3 | 4 | 5 | 6 | 7 | 8 | 9 |
| 10 | 11 | 12 | 13 | 14 | 15 | 16 |
| 17 | 18 | 19 | 20 | 21 | 22 | 23 |
| 24 | 25 | 26 | 27 | 28 | 29 | 30 |
| 31 |   |   |   |   |   |   |

## SEPTEMBER
| M | T | W | T | F | S | S |
|---|---|---|---|---|---|---|
|   | 1 | 2 | 3 | 4 | 5 | 6 |
| 7 | 8 | 9 | 10 | 11 | 12 | 13 |
| 14 | 15 | 16 | 17 | 18 | 19 | 20 |
| 21 | 22 | 23 | 24 | 25 | 26 | 27 |
| 28 | 29 | 30 |   |   |   |   |

## OCTOBER
| M | T | W | T | F | S | S |
|---|---|---|---|---|---|---|
|   |   |   | 1 | 2 | 3 | 4 |
| 5 | 6 | 7 | 8 | 9 | 10 | 11 |
| 12 | 13 | 14 | 15 | 16 | 17 | 18 |
| 19 | 20 | 21 | 22 | 23 | 24 | 25 |
| 26 | 27 | 28 | 29 | 30 | 31 |   |

## NOVEMBER
| M | T | W | T | F | S | S |
|---|---|---|---|---|---|---|
|   |   |   |   |   |   | 1 |
| 2 | 3 | 4 | 5 | 6 | 7 | 8 |
| 9 | 10 | 11 | 12 | 13 | 14 | 15 |
| 16 | 17 | 18 | 19 | 20 | 21 | 22 |
| 23 | 24 | 25 | 26 | 27 | 28 | 29 |
| 30 |   |   |   |   |   |   |

## DECEMBER
| M | T | W | T | F | S | S |
|---|---|---|---|---|---|---|
|   | 1 | 2 | 3 | 4 | 5 | 6 |
| 7 | 8 | 9 | 10 | 11 | 12 | 13 |
| 14 | 15 | 16 | 17 | 18 | 19 | 20 |
| 21 | 22 | 23 | 24 | 25 | 26 | 27 |
| 28 | 29 | 30 | 31 |   |   |   |

# 2016

## JANUARY
| M | T | W | T | F | S | S |
|---|---|---|---|---|---|---|
|   |   |   |   | 1 | 2 | 3 |
| 4 | 5 | 6 | 7 | 8 | 9 | 10 |
| 11 | 12 | 13 | 14 | 15 | 16 | 17 |
| 18 | 19 | 20 | 21 | 22 | 23 | 24 |
| 25 | 26 | 27 | 28 | 29 | 30 | 31 |

## FEBRUARY
| M | T | W | T | F | S | S |
|---|---|---|---|---|---|---|
| 1 | 2 | 3 | 4 | 5 | 6 | 7 |
| 8 | 9 | 10 | 11 | 12 | 13 | 14 |
| 15 | 16 | 17 | 18 | 19 | 20 | 21 |
| 22 | 23 | 24 | 25 | 26 | 27 | 28 |
| 29 |   |   |   |   |   |   |

## MARCH
| M | T | W | T | F | S | S |
|---|---|---|---|---|---|---|
|   | 1 | 2 | 3 | 4 | 5 | 6 |
| 7 | 8 | 9 | 10 | 11 | 12 | 13 |
| 14 | 15 | 16 | 17 | 18 | 19 | 20 |
| 21 | 22 | 23 | 24 | 25 | 26 | 27 |
| 28 | 29 | 30 | 31 |   |   |   |

## APRIL
| M | T | W | T | F | S | S |
|---|---|---|---|---|---|---|
|   |   |   |   | 1 | 2 | 3 |
| 4 | 5 | 6 | 7 | 8 | 9 | 10 |
| 11 | 12 | 13 | 14 | 15 | 16 | 17 |
| 18 | 19 | 20 | 21 | 22 | 23 | 24 |
| 25 | 26 | 27 | 28 | 29 | 30 |   |

## MAY
| M | T | W | T | F | S | S |
|---|---|---|---|---|---|---|
|   |   |   |   |   |   | 1 |
| 2 | 3 | 4 | 5 | 6 | 7 | 8 |
| 9 | 10 | 11 | 12 | 13 | 14 | 15 |
| 16 | 17 | 18 | 19 | 20 | 21 | 22 |
| 23 | 24 | 25 | 26 | 27 | 28 | 29 |
| 30 | 31 |   |   |   |   |   |

## JUNE
| M | T | W | T | F | S | S |
|---|---|---|---|---|---|---|
|   |   | 1 | 2 | 3 | 4 | 5 |
| 6 | 7 | 8 | 9 | 10 | 11 | 12 |
| 13 | 14 | 15 | 16 | 17 | 18 | 19 |
| 20 | 21 | 22 | 23 | 24 | 25 | 26 |
| 27 | 28 | 29 | 30 |   |   |   |

## JULY
| M | T | W | T | F | S | S |
|---|---|---|---|---|---|---|
|   |   |   |   | 1 | 2 | 3 |
| 4 | 5 | 6 | 7 | 8 | 9 | 10 |
| 11 | 12 | 13 | 14 | 15 | 16 | 17 |
| 18 | 19 | 20 | 21 | 22 | 23 | 24 |
| 25 | 26 | 27 | 28 | 29 | 30 | 31 |

## AUGUST
| M | T | W | T | F | S | S |
|---|---|---|---|---|---|---|
| 1 | 2 | 3 | 4 | 5 | 6 | 7 |
| 8 | 9 | 10 | 11 | 12 | 13 | 14 |
| 15 | 16 | 17 | 18 | 19 | 20 | 21 |
| 22 | 23 | 24 | 25 | 26 | 27 | 28 |
| 29 | 30 | 31 |   |   |   |   |

## SEPTEMBER
| M | T | W | T | F | S | S |
|---|---|---|---|---|---|---|
|   |   |   | 1 | 2 | 3 | 4 |
| 5 | 6 | 7 | 8 | 9 | 10 | 11 |
| 12 | 13 | 14 | 15 | 16 | 17 | 18 |
| 19 | 20 | 21 | 22 | 23 | 24 | 25 |
| 26 | 27 | 28 | 29 | 30 |   |   |

## OCTOBER
| M | T | W | T | F | S | S |
|---|---|---|---|---|---|---|
|   |   |   |   |   | 1 | 2 |
| 3 | 4 | 5 | 6 | 7 | 8 | 9 |
| 10 | 11 | 12 | 13 | 14 | 15 | 16 |
| 17 | 18 | 19 | 20 | 21 | 22 | 23 |
| 24 | 25 | 26 | 27 | 28 | 29 | 30 |
| 31 |   |   |   |   |   |   |

## NOVEMBER
| M | T | W | T | F | S | S |
|---|---|---|---|---|---|---|
|   | 1 | 2 | 3 | 4 | 5 | 6 |
| 7 | 8 | 9 | 10 | 11 | 12 | 13 |
| 14 | 15 | 16 | 17 | 18 | 19 | 20 |
| 21 | 22 | 23 | 24 | 25 | 26 | 27 |
| 28 | 29 | 30 |   |   |   |   |

## DECEMBER
| M | T | W | T | F | S | S |
|---|---|---|---|---|---|---|
|   |   |   | 1 | 2 | 3 | 4 |
| 5 | 6 | 7 | 8 | 9 | 10 | 11 |
| 12 | 13 | 14 | 15 | 16 | 17 | 18 |
| 19 | 20 | 21 | 22 | 23 | 24 | 25 |
| 26 | 27 | 28 | 29 | 30 | 31 |   |

# 2017

## JANUARY
| M | T | W | T | F | S | S |
|---|---|---|---|---|---|---|
|   |   |   |   |   |   | 1 |
| 2 | 3 | 4 | 5 | 6 | 7 | 8 |
| 9 | 10 | 11 | 12 | 13 | 14 | 15 |
| 16 | 17 | 18 | 19 | 20 | 21 | 22 |
| 23 | 24 | 25 | 26 | 27 | 28 | 29 |
| 30 | 31 |   |   |   |   |   |

## FEBRUARY
| M | T | W | T | F | S | S |
|---|---|---|---|---|---|---|
|   |   | 1 | 2 | 3 | 4 | 5 |
| 6 | 7 | 8 | 9 | 10 | 11 | 12 |
| 13 | 14 | 15 | 16 | 17 | 18 | 19 |
| 20 | 21 | 22 | 23 | 24 | 25 | 26 |
| 27 | 28 |   |   |   |   |   |

## MARCH
| M | T | W | T | F | S | S |
|---|---|---|---|---|---|---|
|   |   | 1 | 2 | 3 | 4 | 5 |
| 6 | 7 | 8 | 9 | 10 | 11 | 12 |
| 13 | 14 | 15 | 16 | 17 | 18 | 19 |
| 20 | 21 | 22 | 23 | 24 | 25 | 26 |
| 27 | 28 | 29 | 30 | 31 |   |   |

## APRIL
| M | T | W | T | F | S | S |
|---|---|---|---|---|---|---|
|   |   |   |   |   | 1 | 2 |
| 3 | 4 | 5 | 6 | 7 | 8 | 9 |
| 10 | 11 | 12 | 13 | 14 | 15 | 16 |
| 17 | 18 | 19 | 20 | 21 | 22 | 23 |
| 24 | 25 | 26 | 27 | 28 | 29 | 30 |

## MAY
| M | T | W | T | F | S | S |
|---|---|---|---|---|---|---|
| 1 | 2 | 3 | 4 | 5 | 6 | 7 |
| 8 | 9 | 10 | 11 | 12 | 13 | 14 |
| 15 | 16 | 17 | 18 | 19 | 20 | 21 |
| 22 | 23 | 24 | 25 | 26 | 27 | 28 |
| 29 | 30 | 31 |   |   |   |   |

## JUNE
| M | T | W | T | F | S | S |
|---|---|---|---|---|---|---|
|   |   |   | 1 | 2 | 3 | 4 |
| 5 | 6 | 7 | 8 | 9 | 10 | 11 |
| 12 | 13 | 14 | 15 | 16 | 17 | 18 |
| 19 | 20 | 21 | 22 | 23 | 24 | 25 |
| 26 | 27 | 28 | 29 | 30 |   |   |

## JULY
| M | T | W | T | F | S | S |
|---|---|---|---|---|---|---|
|   |   |   |   |   | 1 | 2 |
| 3 | 4 | 5 | 6 | 7 | 8 | 9 |
| 10 | 11 | 12 | 13 | 14 | 15 | 16 |
| 17 | 18 | 19 | 20 | 21 | 22 | 23 |
| 24 | 25 | 26 | 27 | 28 | 29 | 30 |
| 31 |   |   |   |   |   |   |

## AUGUST
| M | T | W | T | F | S | S |
|---|---|---|---|---|---|---|
|   | 1 | 2 | 3 | 4 | 5 | 6 |
| 7 | 8 | 9 | 10 | 11 | 12 | 13 |
| 14 | 15 | 16 | 17 | 18 | 19 | 20 |
| 21 | 22 | 23 | 24 | 25 | 26 | 27 |
| 28 | 29 | 30 | 31 |   |   |   |

## SEPTEMBER
| M | T | W | T | F | S | S |
|---|---|---|---|---|---|---|
|   |   |   |   | 1 | 2 | 3 |
| 4 | 5 | 6 | 7 | 8 | 9 | 10 |
| 11 | 12 | 13 | 14 | 15 | 16 | 17 |
| 18 | 19 | 20 | 21 | 22 | 23 | 24 |
| 25 | 26 | 27 | 28 | 29 | 30 |   |

## OCTOBER
| M | T | W | T | F | S | S |
|---|---|---|---|---|---|---|
|   |   |   |   |   |   | 1 |
| 2 | 3 | 4 | 5 | 6 | 7 | 8 |
| 9 | 10 | 11 | 12 | 13 | 14 | 15 |
| 16 | 17 | 18 | 19 | 20 | 21 | 22 |
| 23 | 24 | 25 | 26 | 27 | 28 | 29 |
| 30 | 31 |   |   |   |   |   |

## NOVEMBER
| M | T | W | T | F | S | S |
|---|---|---|---|---|---|---|
|   |   | 1 | 2 | 3 | 4 | 5 |
| 6 | 7 | 8 | 9 | 10 | 11 | 12 |
| 13 | 14 | 15 | 16 | 17 | 18 | 19 |
| 20 | 21 | 22 | 23 | 24 | 25 | 26 |
| 27 | 28 | 29 | 30 |   |   |   |

## DECEMBER
| M | T | W | T | F | S | S |
|---|---|---|---|---|---|---|
|   |   |   |   | 1 | 2 | 3 |
| 4 | 5 | 6 | 7 | 8 | 9 | 10 |
| 11 | 12 | 13 | 14 | 15 | 16 | 17 |
| 18 | 19 | 20 | 21 | 22 | 23 | 24 |
| 25 | 26 | 27 | 28 | 29 | 30 | 31 |

# Three Year Planner

2015

2016

2017

# Addresses

Name:  
Address:  


Telephone:  
Email:  

Name:  
Address:  


Telephone:  
Email:  

Name:  
Address:  


Telephone:  
Email:  

Name:  
Address:  


Telephone:  
Email:  

Name:  
Address:  


Telephone:  
Email:  

Name:  
Address:  


Telephone:  
Email:  

Name:  
Address:  


Telephone:  
Email:  

Name:  
Address:  


Telephone:  
Email:  

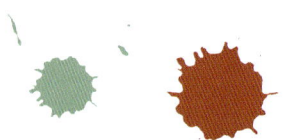

Name:
Address:


Telephone:
Email:

Name:
Address:


Telephone:
Email:

Name:
Address:


Telephone:
Email:

Name:
Address:


Telephone:
Email:

Name:
Address:


Telephone:
Email:

Name:
Address:


Telephone:
Email:

Name:
Address:


Telephone:
Email:

Name:
Address:


Telephone:
Email:

# Notes

# Notes

**A DAVID & CHARLES BOOK**
© F&W Media International, Ltd 2013

David & Charles is an imprint of F&W Media International, Ltd
Brunel House, Forde Close, Newton Abbot, TQ12 4PU, UK

F&W Media International, Ltd is a subsidiary of F+W Media, Inc
10151 Carver Road, Suite #200 Blue Ash, OH 45242, USA

Text, layout and photography © F&W Media International, Ltd 2013

First published in the UK and USA in 2013

All rights reserved. No part of this publication may be reproduced in any form or by any means, electronic or mechanical, by photocopying, recording or otherwise, without prior permission in writing from the publisher.

A catalogue record for this book is available from the British Library.

ISBN-13: 978-1-4463-0364-1 hardback
ISBN-10: 1-4463-0364-0 hardback

Printed in China by Toppan Leefung Printing Limited for:
F&W Media International, Ltd
Brunel House, Forde Close, Newton Abbot, TQ12 4PU, UK

F+W Media publishes high quality books on a wide range of subjects.
For more great book ideas visit: **www.stitchcraftcreate.co.uk**